# The Pedagogy of Real Talk

*I dedicate this book to my momma, educators, and students. Momma, you are the good people see in my eyes and you are what this world needs. Educators, you wield extraordinary power to empower students to achieve their dreams as you helped me achieve my own. Students, you have a voice and should be heard in a world that you, I hope, will shape for the better.*

# The Pedagogy of Real Talk

## Engaging, Teaching, and
## Connecting With Students at Risk

**Paul Hernandez**

*Foreword by David Osher*

FOR INFORMATION:

Corwin

A SAGE Company

2455 Teller Road

Thousand Oaks, California 91320

(800) 233-9936

www.corwin.com

SAGE Publications Ltd.

1 Oliver's Yard

55 City Road

London EC1Y 1SP

United Kingdom

SAGE Publications India Pvt. Ltd.

B 1/I 1 Mohan Cooperative Industrial Area

Mathura Road, New Delhi 110 044

India

SAGE Publications Asia-Pacific Pte. Ltd.

3 Church Street

#10-04 Samsung Hub

Singapore 049483

Senior Acquisitions Editor:  Jessica Allan

Senior Associate Editor:  Kimberly Greenberg

Editorial Assistant:  Cesar Reyes

Production Editor:  Veronica Stapleton Hooper

Copy Editor:  Matthew Connor Sullivan

Typesetter:  C&M Digitals (P) Ltd.

Proofreader:  Annie Lubinsky

Indexer:  Jean Casalegno

Cover Designer:  Eve King

Marketing Manager:  Stephanie Trkay

Printed in the United States of America

*A catalog record of this book is available from the Library of Congress.*

ISBN 978-1-4833-7711-7

This book is printed on acid-free paper.

15 16 17 18 19 10 9 8 7 6 5 4 3 2 1

# *Contents*

**Foreword**　　　　　　　　　　　　　　　　　　　　viii
*David Osher*

**Preface**　　　　　　　　　　　　　　　　　　　　　　xi

**Acknowledgments**　　　　　　　　　　　　　　　　xiv

**About the Author**　　　　　　　　　　　　　　　　xv

**Chapter 1 Introduction**　　　　　　　　　　　　　1
Students at Risk　　　　　　　　　　　　　　　　　　2
The Researcher　　　　　　　　　　　　　　　　　　5
MSU HEP　　　　　　　　　　　　　　　　　　　　　6
The Pedagogy　　　　　　　　　　　　　　　　　　　8

**Chapter 2 Real Talk**　　　　　　　　　　　　　　10
The Theoretical Foundations of Real Talk　　　　　10
Refinement of the Pedagogy of Real Talk　　　　　15
The Pedagogy of Real Talk and Other Approaches　21

**Chapter 3 The Students, Their Experiences,**
**   and the Academic Results**　　　　　　　　　　24
Inception of the Case Study　　　　　　　　　　　　25
HEP Student Participants　　　　　　　　　　　　　26
The Results　　　　　　　　　　　　　　　　　　　40

**Chapter 4 Implementing Real Talk in the HEP Program**　45
Dialogue　　　　　　　　　　　　　　　　　　　　46
Relating to Students　　　　　　　　　　　　　　　47
Structure　　　　　　　　　　　　　　　　　　　　48
Clarity　　　　　　　　　　　　　　　　　　　　　50
Redundancy　　　　　　　　　　　　　　　　　　　51
Enthusiasm　　　　　　　　　　　　　　　　　　　54
Appropriate Pace　　　　　　　　　　　　　　　　　55
Maximized Engagement　　　　　　　　　　　　　　56

**Chapter 5 Flexibility, Adaptability, and Effort**          **59**
   Flexibility                                                60
   Adaptability                                               62
   Effort                                                     64

**Chapter 6 Terministic Screens and Real Talk Discussions**  **66**
   Terministic Screens                                        66
   Real Talk                                                  69

**Chapter 7 Dealing With the Exceptions**                    **77**
   The Case of PB                                             77
   The Case of Jessie                                         79
   The Case of LB                                             81
   The Challenge to Teachers                                  82

**Chapter 8 Implementing Real Talk in Any Classroom**        **85**

**Chapter 9 The Training of Teachers**                       **88**
   The Basic Components and Foundations of the Pedagogy        91
   Connections Through Real Talk                              92
   Another Real Talk Example                                  98
   Maintaining Connections                                    101

**Chapter 10 Training: Alternative Lessons**                 **104**
   Alternative Lesson Examples                                107

**Chapter 11 Training and Feedback**                         **116**

**Chapter 12 New Beginnings**                                **121**

**Appendices**                                               **126**

**Appendix A Real Talk on Symbolism**                        **128**

**Appendix B "Who I Am" Real Talk on the First Day of Class** **131**

**Appendix C Real Talk on Adversity**                        **133**

**Appendix D Real Talk on Assumptions**                      **136**

**Appendix E Real Talk on Overcoming Personal
   Challenges With Hard Work and Determination**              **138**

**Appendix F Real Talk on Transforming Frustration and
   Anger Into Empowerment**                                   **140**

**Appendix G Real Talk on Being Authentic**                  **144**

**Appendix H Real Talk on Classroom Norms**                  **146**

**Appendix I Examples of Real Talk Themes**                  **148**

Appendix J Bridge Project Packet                                    150

Appendix K Alternative Lesson on Congruent Triangles                161

Appendix L Alternative Lesson on Federal Courts
    and the Judicial Branch                                     168

Appendix M Alternative Lesson on Graphing
    Different Types of Linear Systems                            172

Appendix N Alternative Lesson on Public Speaking Anxiety            179

Appendix O Alternative Lesson Topics and Summaries                  181

Appendix P Games                                                    183

Bibliography                                                        185

Index                                                               188

# *Foreword*

Risk and well-being are socially constructed, and schools play a key role in the dynamic processes that contribute to school failure and success, as well as to inegalitarian and egalitarian outcomes. Students whom educators often view or label as being "at risk" are children and youth first and foremost. Like other students whom we see as "at promise," they, too, are at promise. However, they need positive conditions for learning—emotional and physical safety, connectedness and care, and academic challenge and support (Osher & Kendziora, 2010)—as well as social and emotional learning and talent development. Like other learners, they have lives, experiences, interests, and desires that contextualize and drive their learning. And like other adolescents, they have needs, and these include respect, agency, voice, a sense of belonging, caring relationships with adults, and engagement (Eccles & Roser, 2011). However, students who are at risk often need personalized, strength-based, culturally competent services and supports that address barriers to learning, and these are often woefully absent.

Although important, services and supports are likely to be insufficient—young people who are at risk also need supportive school environments. Many students who are at risk are more sensitive to environmental toxicities than their peers and require even stronger universal conditions for learning than their peers (Osher, Sidana, & Kelly, 2008; Osher et al., under review). Unfortunately, these students often feel less safe, less supported, and less challenged and supported academically than their less challenged peers (Osher & Kendziora, 2011; Spier, Garibaldi, & Osher, 2012). They often view school as aversive, particularly when they (along with others who look like them) experience academic tracking, demoralized and disempowered teachers, and punitive and exclusionary discipline. They sense micro-agression rather than respect; external control rather than autonomy; imposed silence (including when they are not called upon or are given less wait time, Osher et al., 2004) rather than voice; rejection and exclusionary discipline rather than care, inclusion, and invitations to participate; and learned helplessness rather than growth mindsets and school-related efficacy. Not surprisingly, these students often report academic frustration, boredom, and irrelevance rather than engagement. Like the young Paul Hernandez, they often feel like imposters, and their negative experiences push them away from academic learning and school and toward oppositional cultures both in school and on the streets.

Students are not passive victims here. They use their agency to resist—both actively and passively—the imposition of alienating demands. As Paul Hernandez reflected: "I exercised my only form of power in the classroom as a student: resisting the teacher at the expense of my own success." In their attempts to create and maintain their own sense of autonomy, dignity, and safety they often act tough and demonstrate little respect for school norms and adult authority. Although this resistance may feel good to youth in the short run, it further alienates them from learning, reinforces the oppositional behavior of their peers, and evokes counteraggressive behavior of adults. These consequences are educationally and socially portentous as they contribute to the reproduction and legitimation of both educational inequities and education-based inequality (Ogbu & Davis, 1983; Willis, 1981).

Students, however, are not alone here. The inability of many educators to establish caring and respectful relationships with students contributes to student disconnection. Moreover, their overreliance on external discipline and formal authority exacerbates alienation and escalates resistance. These challenges, however, can be addressed, and Paul Hernandez provides part of a road map through his conceptualization and operationalization of the Pedagogy of Real Talk—integrating into the classrooms instructor-led discussion surrounding a series of broad, engaging universal themes designed to motivate student-oriented outcomes and to establish connections, understanding, trust, empathy, and caring between and among students and teachers. While doing this Hernandez aligns pedagogical approaches that are often un- or under-aligned: liberatory approaches to education that address student experience and voice, effective approaches to differentiating instruction and scaffolding learning, and developing teacher attribute and skills.

Individual teachers can do this work, as demonstrated by teachers who effectively implement the ideas of such influential pedagogical thinkers as Mike Rose (1995), John Dewey (1902), Paulo Freire (who was influenced by Dewey, among others, 1970), Ira Shor (who applied Freire to teaching in the U.S., 1992), Lev Vygotsky (1978), and Nicolas Hobbs (1982). However, if these approaches are to affect most students who are at risk, it is important to systemically build teacher capacity as well as positive conditions for learning. It is also important to develop student and teacher social and emotional skills along with students' academic interest and proficiency. Doing this can leverage the potential of The Pedagogy of Real Talk and help build schools where youth drive engagement, and students and teachers collaborate to enhance student and faculty learning and well-being.

# REFERENCES

Dewey, J. *The Child and the Curriculum*, Chicago: University of Chicago Press, 1902.

Eccles, J., and R. Roeser. "Schools as Developmental Contexts During Adolescence." *Journal of Research on Adolescence* (n.d.): 225–241.

Freire, P. *Pedagogy of the Oppressed.* New York: Continuum, 1970.

Hobbs, N. *The Troubled and Troubling Child*. San Francisco: Jossey-Bass, 1982.

Ogbu, J. *Black American Students in an Affluent Suburb: A Study of Academic Disengagement*. Mahwah, New Jersey: L. Erlbaum Associates, 2003.

Osher, D., Y. Kidron, C. J. DeCandia, K. Kendziora, and R. Weissberg. "Interventions to Promote Safe and Supportive School Climate." In K. Wentzel and G. Ramani, eds. *Handbook of Social Influences on Social-Emotional, Motivation, and Cognitive Outcomes in School Contexts*, under review.

Osher, D., K. Kendziora, E. Spier, and M. L. Garibaldi. "School Influences on Child and Youth Development." In Z. Sloboda and H. Petras, eds. *Advances in Prevention Science Vol. 1: Defining Prevention Science.* New York: Springer, 2014.

Osher, D., and K. Kendziora. "Building Conditions for Learning and Healthy Adolescent Development: Strategic Approaches." in B. Doll, W. Pfohl, and J. Yoon, eds. *Handbook of Youth Prevention Science (pp 121–140).* New York: Rutledge, 2010.

Osher, D., K. Dwyer, and S. Jackson. *Safe, Supportive, and Successful Schools Step by Step.* Longmont, CO: Sopris West, 2004.

Osher, D., A. Sidana, and P. Kelly. *Improving Conditions for Learning for Youth Who Are Neglected or Delinquent.* Washington, D.C.: National Evaluation and Technical Assistance Center for the Education of Children and Youth who are Delinquent, Neglected, or at Risk, 2008.

Rose, M. *Lives on the Boundary.* New York: Free Press, 1989.

Shore, I. *Empowering Education: Critical Teaching for Social Change.* Chicago: University of Chicago Press, 1992.

Spier, E., M. Garibaldi, and D. Osher. Alaska School Climate and Connectedness: Listening to the Voices of Connected and Disconnected Alaskan Native and Non-Alaskan Native Youth. Washington, D. C.: American Institutes for Research, 2012.

Vygotsky, L. *Mind in Society: The Development of Higher Psychological Processes.* Cambridge, MA: Harvard University Press, 1978.

Willis, P. *Learning to Labor: How Working Class Kids Get Working Class Jobs.* NY: Columbia University Press, 1981.

David Osher, Ph.D.

Vice President

Senior Advisor to the Health and Social Development Program

American Institutes for Research

# *Preface*

I remember as if it were yesterday, the day my life changed forever. I was a kid from the streets of Los Angeles who was not supposed to live to see my 16th birthday, let alone achieve any level of personal success. I was engulfed in the gang life, living in constant threat and turmoil, with hate, bitterness, and so much pain. Growing weary of this life, I posed a simple question to the older homeboys, "Why are things the way they are for us?" Their answer was, "It is what it is." After several months of wrestling with their response, the answer came to me clearly. You see, I realized that the answer isn't simply, "It is what it is" but instead, "It is what it is . . . because someone made it that way." That meant I could change things. This epiphany began the transformation of my life.

I went from a disengaged, standoffish, apathetic, disruptive student who seldom went to school to a young man who embraced education and recognized it as a source of empowerment that would help me change the world for the better. Never having known anyone who had graduated from high school made the journey a mysterious and scary process. But thanks to a handful of wonderful educators—from the custodian in elementary school who taught me I was not a monster, to my mentor, Dr. Wasson, who guided me through undergraduate studies and into graduate school—I learned the necessary skills to allow me to be successful in school. I felt like quitting many times. However, my momma's words echoed through my mind, along with images of my homeboys who had lost their lives or were locked away in prison and the voices of the people who said I would never amount to anything in life. These all further strengthened what my momma called my belief muscle—the belief that through my efforts and struggles I could achieve the unimaginable for a kid like me, and it was my responsibility to not let this belief weaken.

During graduate school, I worked as an adjunct instructor at a community college and taught General Educational Development (GED) courses at a university. I was fortunate to then be offered a tenure-track faculty position. This allowed me a platform to teach courses, conduct research, and create programs through service. I was incredibly humbled to be awarded Honors Professor of the Year for my teaching and a National Human and Civil Rights Award for a program I created that has served thousands of students considered at risk of dropping out of school. As I progressed as a faculty member, I came to a point where I wanted to further evolve and contribute to the success of professionals working with students and communities. I transitioned from my professorial role to working with universities, community colleges, high schools, and nonprofit organizations around the country. Through my pedagogy, I helped develop, assess, and restructure educational initiatives; created programming; conducted workshops; delivered keynotes; and trained educators, administrators, and others in my approach. I am extremely fortunate that I have had and continue to have opportunities to contribute to the success of so many institutions and organizations attempting to empower students.

This book is something that I created from a moral and professional obligation. I have experienced the hardships and challenges of being in the classroom as both a student and a teacher. I decided that instead of becoming cynical, I would create something new from the standpoint of a former dropout, researcher, and educator to assure that I could contribute further to the success of dedicated professionals and the students they serve. Although the foundations of this book took root in a GED program, they have evolved and been successful with thousands of higher education, K–12, and nonprofit professionals I have trained in using, applying, and modifying this approach. Others' implementation of the pedagogy in a plethora of classroom types and environments has contributed to the evolution of the approach to what it has become today, the focus of this book.[1]

The Pedagogy of Real Talk was created for use either in its entirety or in conjunction with other approaches. Flexibility is essential, as teaching should not follow a rigid cookie-cutter approach. The pedagogy is built to provide a research-based foundation with applicable, practical tools for the reader to use according to his or her individual personality and style. Additionally, I wanted to provide a resource that supports the fact that relevancy, connections, and relationships with students matter when attempting to teach them. I view teaching as an art form that takes time to master. I have aimed to supply individuals with another tool to paint their masterpieces through the success of their students and fulfillment within their careers.

It is my hope that this book will support the beginnings of a paradigm shift in teaching and learning within our educational system. Teaching is not a method to control students, impose perspectives on them, or merely prepare them to pass a test. Teaching is the creation of an environment that is conducive to learning, one in which we offer students the opportunity

---

[1]Although I most often refer to teachers, this is something that can be used by instructors, professors, or any other professional in a classroom with students.

to learn the necessary skills to pass tests, prepare for the workforce, and ensure that they have as many options as possible for their futures. Teaching needs to allow students to be heard and create an inviting space where students want to be instead of where they have to be. Teaching our students means getting to know them; otherwise, how can we possibly teach them? We are powerful educators who have the opportunity to empower lives.

I fully expect that through the brilliant minds who engage in this pedagogy, this approach will further evolve. Thank you to those who embrace or challenge it. I remember words of wisdom from my momma (translated from Spanish): "Remember that you will never reach the pinnacle. You will always grow and learn new things throughout the rest of your life. You will only stop growing when you stop caring." Therefore, I leave you with *The Pedagogy of Real Talk,* an approach created to support all who care about our students and their future.

# *Acknowledgments*

I would like to offer my warmest gratitude to Karla and Wasson for believing in me, pushing me when I felt like I couldn't take another step forward, and never doubting what my ideas could become. Additionally, I am grateful to Dori, Katie, David, and Tommy for implementing and living the pedagogy and helping me to further evolve in my work to better serve students.

## PUBLISHER'S ACKNOWLEDGMENTS

Corwin gratefully acknowledges the contributions of the following reviewers.

Dano Beal, Teacher,
Advanced Learning Seattle
   Schools
Seattle Public Schools
Seattle, WA

Elizabeth H. Bradley, Assistant
   Principal
Lewiston High School
Lewiston, Maine

Dr. Rich Hall, Principal
Henrico County Public Schools
Henrico, VA

Scott Hollinger,
University Professor;
   Instructional Coach
Teachers College Columbia
   University
New York, NY

Nicola Labas, Principal
SDUSD
Imperial Beach, CA

# *About the Author*

**Paul Hernandez, PhD,** earned his doctorate in sociology specializing in the sociology of education, social inequality, and diversity. Dr. Hernandez is a nationally recognized speaker and leader in college access and success, community outreach, and pedagogy for educators working with underserved/underprepared students and students at risk of dropping out of school. As a former faculty member, nonprofit administrator, and educational consultant, Dr. Hernandez works with higher education institutions, K–12 schools, and nonprofit organizations, helping them further develop and evolve their work with students and communities. Prior to earning his degrees, he was engulfed in gang culture and deep poverty, surviving on the streets of Los Angeles. Paul openly shares with others his unique personal story of being a youth at risk and how his path has influenced his work. He has learned ways to empower young people traveling a similar path, and through his inspirational messages hopes to share his lessons and passion with those working to address the multitude of challenges faced by diverse populations of youth at risk. Dr. Hernandez was awarded the National Education Association Reg Weaver Human and Civil Rights Award, the Michigan Education Association Elizabeth Siddall Human Rights Award, the Equity in Education Award by the Michigan Association of Collegiate Registrars and Admissions Officers, and an Honors Professor of the Year Award for teaching.

# 1

## *Introduction*

**W**hen I was struggling in high school, administrators and teachers often spoke of me as a thing rather than as a person. They struggled to connect with me and my homeboys or to help us see a world beyond the Los Angeles ghettos. Rather than trying alternative methods to connect with students like us, teachers and administrators simply punished us and considered us a burden in the classroom. Eventually, I simply stopped going to school because education became my enemy rather than a source of empowerment to better my life. The feminization of deep poverty,[1] hunger, gangs, violence, and the social stigma of being different all contributed to my downward spiral within the education system. The manner in which I viewed the world and understood society, along with what I experienced on a day-to-day basis, was simply disregarded in the classroom. I was another student at risk destined to drop out of school.

These experiences instilled a passion within me to create an alternative pedagogy to empower teachers to become more successful in working with students at risk and, in turn, to increase passing rates for these students. I went from detesting school as a student at risk to attaining my PhD. Today my experience serves as a testament to the potential of students at risk and as a reminder for teachers not to give up on their most challenging students.

Although academic success is crucial to being successful in American society, getting a job, owning a home, and reaching the middle class, students at risk find succeeding in school difficult, if not impossible.

---

[1]The feminization of deep poverty refers to the disproportionate percentage of households headed by single females living 50% below the poverty level.

The negative experiences these students have in school and in their communities contribute to their poor performance, and their lack of academic success limits their opportunities for employment and educational growth. On a larger scale, their lack of success weakens the country overall. The nation needs more college-educated people to fill or to create much-needed jobs. Helping this population succeed is a major obstacle for teachers, a seemingly elusive goal—a goal that must be met!

However, in all the discussions centered on students at risk, relevant solutions are rarely offered to teachers. Instead, the focus is on the conditions that lead to failure: the students' environment and the disadvantages they experience that result in their failure in school. Although it is important to identify these foundational issues to help students succeed, simply identifying them without creating applicable solutions for educators to incorporate in their classrooms is an injustice to teachers and students everywhere. Some even believe students at risk do not want to learn, as reflected in one teacher's questions: "How do I teach students who do not seem to want to learn? How do I show them the importance of school when it seems like school just doesn't fit in with their lives?" Meanwhile, students at risk mistakenly believe that school is not for them and that educators do not care about them.

My answer to this dilemma is the Pedagogy of Real Talk. Teachers can come to class with great ideas, interesting statistics, fascinating movies, and the coolest stories, but if there is no connection with this population of students, these approaches will fall on deaf ears because the students will not be receptive. Through the Pedagogy of Real Talk, teachers and students connect with curriculum through real-life experiences, allowing teachers to establish meaningful connections with students. As a result, students at risk become receptive to learning from their teachers. The Pedagogy of Real Talk allows teachers to gain valuable insights into their students, something not usually possible with traditional approaches. As students become responsive to learning and as teachers gain insight into their students, the pedagogy then helps teachers create alternative lessons and assignments that connect students with the curriculum. The barriers between teachers and students at risk crumble as new and exciting environments conducive to learning emerge to increase passing rates for students at risk.

## STUDENTS AT RISK

Almost any student may be categorized as at risk under the right circumstances. For the purposes of this book, I have chosen the definition provided by Stormont and Thomas:[2]

---

[2]As quoted in Melissa Stormont and Cathy Newman Thomas, *Simple Strategies for Teaching Children at Risk* (Thousand Oaks, CA: Corwin, 2014), 3; see also 5, Figure 1.1.

> Students who are at-risk for failure [or dropping out of school] include students who have within [person] and/or within environmental circumstances that put them in vulnerable positions for having problems in school. These problems can be academic or social or both. Within person risk factors include [but are not limited to] ADHD, no or limited knowledge/skills or [social, emotional, and behavior problems]. [Some examples of] environmental risks include poverty-homelessness, limited support for learning, [gangs, drugs,] and negative interactions at school, home, or between school and home.

But it is important to keep in mind that being at risk of failure or dropping out does not mean students are bound to fail or drop out.

Common characteristics of students at risk include low self-confidence with schoolwork, avoidance of school, distrust of adults, and limited notions of their academic future. They often present behavioral problems in the classroom that disrupt the learning process for themselves and others. Many teachers describe these students as burdens in the classroom and feel hopeless in trying to teach them successfully.

Students at risk often have fragile home lives and may drop out or be forced out of the educational system because of various life circumstances. A majority of students at risk live in low-income households, meaning they have limited resources, social capital, and parental guidance. They often live in poor, dilapidated neighborhoods plagued with crime and violence. Reduced levels of supervision increase the likelihood of their involvement in negative activities that promote their disconnection from classes and loss of interest in school. They are discouraged learners who view success in school as a matter of luck rather than of their intellect and hard work. Conversely, these students may be pushed out because of age, lack of credit transfer between school districts and states, and differences in educational systems between countries.

We must also keep in mind that students within this population are at risk for a variety of reasons. They are not a homogeneous group just because they are all at risk of dropping out of school. Some students are at risk because they have substance abuse problems. Some are bullied. Others are homeless or abused at home. Some work over 40 hours a week in addition to attending school. In other words, a student at risk can be a student who is the son or daughter of a two-parent, upper-middle-class, professional household, or the son or daughter of a poverty-stricken single parent.

Consider these two former students of mine. One student came from a two-parent household. Although both of her parents had college educations and were employed, she was completely disengaged from school, feeling it was a waste of time because school was extremely boring. She failed and dropped out. The other student grew up very poor. He lived with his grandmother rather than with either of his parents. He found it difficult to balance school with his responsibilities at home. To complicate things further, he became a teenage father and eventually dropped out of school. Two very different scenarios with the same unfortunate result: dropping out. Thus, despite their commonality of being at risk of dropping out of school, students at risk are in that position for a variety of personal and environmental reasons.

As teachers, we must remember that students at risk are people before they are students. Only by accepting this first can we expect to work with this population of students effectively. The life experiences these students have outside of school and the problems they face daily, which we often disregard as irrelevant to the classroom, permeate their success in the classroom. Lacking family members or loved ones with education or with real-life examples of people with degrees makes envisioning success in school difficult for students at risk. They struggle to see school as an arena for improving their lives. School is a long-term investment, but their economic needs are immediate and cannot wait until later to be resolved. Because of their economic needs, students at risk may view education as an obstacle or a waste of time. The issues of violence, gangs, drugs, and overall danger that surround or engulf students at risk also detract from students' undivided attention to schoolwork, both in and out of the classroom.

As working professionals, we know that major obstacles within our personal lives impact our performance and ability to succeed in our careers. Why then do we often expect students at risk to be different? Why do we believe their personal lives outside of school should not hinder their ability to succeed in school? Only when we begin to understand the issues our students face can we incorporate what we have learned into meaningful solutions in the classroom to empower our students through education.

According to the Alliance for Excellent Education,[3] only 78% of all high school students graduate. Up to 1.2 million high school students drop out annually. Dropouts earn an average annual income of $19,540 compared with the $27,380 average annual income of high school graduates, a gap of $7,840. This income disparity remains constant for many high school dropouts throughout their lifetimes and contributes to the ongoing cycle of poverty among the children of high school dropouts.

Increasing the success of students at risk by enabling them to graduate high school or college will have profound effects not only for the individual students but also for society in general. We will benefit from reductions in the poverty rate, the increased numbers of educated Americans, and the potential economic benefit based on increased numbers of capable, educated workers. To make any of this feasible, however, we must emphasize and teach educators applicable approaches to build meaningful teacher–student relationships within our educational system.

---

[3]Alliance for Excellent Education, *The High Cost of High School Dropouts: What the Nation Pays for Inadequate High Schools* (Washington, DC: Alliance for Excellent Education, 2011).

# THE RESEARCHER

In developing the Pedagogy of Real Talk, I worked with dropouts who had been accepted into the Michigan State University High School Equivalency Program (MSU HEP). My background is relatively similar to that of many of the students in that program. I grew up within the feminization of deep poverty in this country. I lived engulfed in the street thug lifestyle and was involved with gangs as a youth. I was labeled a student at risk throughout school and dropped out of school multiple times. I continued my education at a community college, earning an associate's degree in liberal arts, and transferred to finish my bachelor's degree in sociology. I then went on to earn a master's degree and PhD in sociology.

I am not just an academic writing a book on an alternative pedagogy but a former student at risk who was supposed to be in prison, dead, or a part of any other statistic within our dropout epidemic. I spent the majority of my life as a young man detesting school, especially the teachers, who I felt were my enemies. I was so entrenched in my views of school that I categorized all teachers as bad, even before I ever encountered them. I did not allow them the opportunity to get to know me—or teach me—the material I was supposed to learn. I took pride in my rejection of school and in the teachers' inability to connect with me. Disturbing class was entertaining to me. More important, when I was forced to be in school, I simply did nothing. I accepted that I would fail because it was more important for me to resist the teacher and reject the teacher's attempts to teach me. Ultimately, I exercised my only form of power in the classroom as a student: resisting the teacher at the expense of my own success.

In middle school, I specifically remember a teacher who told me one day that whenever I showed up to her class, I ruined her day. I was a talkative young man in her class, I admit—but I did not deserve such a spiteful comment, especially from a teacher. It was at that moment that I decided to resist every single thing she would attempt with me to make her feel the disrespect she made me feel. I never brought paper or pencil to her class whenever I attended. I was constantly disruptive, pushing her beyond her limits. She reached her breaking point one day and simply gave me a paper and told me to draw on it. I told her I didn't have something to write with. She responded, "I do not care! Even if you have to write with your blood, you will find something to write with!" I smiled at her and said okay. As she began teaching the class, I cut my finger with my key and wrote my name on the paper in blood. I raised my hand and asked her to come over. "Is this okay?" I asked. I remember how she gasped, eyes nearly exploding. Her face turned a pasty pale complexion, and her body shook as she told me to get out of her class. I remember how good I felt because my sole purpose in that class was to resist her and to make things impossible for her. My extreme actions were a direct result of her comment. I felt most empowered when I resisted and tortured her, even though it was to my detriment. Such problems, which have existed in classrooms for decades, persist in classes today.

Because I have lived through this and been surrounded by countless others who did as well, creating something to help empower teachers in teaching their most challenging students has become my life's passion. I have always felt strongly that the most powerful person in the classroom is the teacher, and that if teachers are taught effective approaches to apply in their classrooms, they can transform the lives of their students in a positive manner. Fusing my academic knowledge as an educator with my own personal insights as the student no teacher could reach, I have created an authentic approach that will resonate with both teachers and students at risk in the classroom.

When I was offered the opportunity to work with students in MSU HEP, I was determined to create and implement an alternative teaching pedagogy to help those students pass their General Educational Development (GED) examination. I have continued to refine and implement that pedagogy and to train other teachers in implementing it successfully in their classrooms and schools.

## MSU HEP

The HEP program at Michigan State University is designed to assist migrant and seasonal farm workers who have not completed high school in obtaining their GEDs.[4] HEP has two main objectives: (1) increasing the percentage of HEP participants who receive their GED diplomas and (2) increasing the percentage of HEP GED recipients placed in postsecondary education programs, upgraded employment, or the military. To be eligible for HEP, students or a member of their immediate families must meet the following requirements:

- Have worked a minimum of 75 days in agriculturally related employment (migrant or seasonal farm work) in the previous 24-month period
- Participate in a Migrant Education Program (Title I, Part C)
- Be eligible for services under the Workforce Investment Act, Section 167 Program;
- Be at least 17 years of age
- Have not received a secondary school diploma

---

[4]The following discussion is based my doctoral dissertation, *Alternative Pedagogy: Empowering Teachers Through Real Talk* (Doctoral dissertation, Michigan State University, 2010), available from ProQuest.

Because admission to the program is based on occupation, no one is excluded based on race or ethnicity. However, the migrant community is a very specific cultural and ethnic demographic, the most common race/ethnicity/culture being Mexican or Mexican American. Therefore, the majority of HEP students are also Mexican or Mexican American

In addition, students who are able to graduate with their high school class (under the age of 16) and students who have received high school diplomas are not eligible for HEP. Most of the participants have either dropped out of school (high school, middle school, and sometimes even elementary school), have been "pushed out" of the system because they lack credits or their credits are nontransferable, or have immigrated to the United States and need an equivalency or certificate of education from the United States. Some have dropped out of school to support their families through migrant or other work. Others have dropped out due to gang involvement, lack of motivation, or discipline or behavior problems. Still others lack any feeling of connection with schools because of conflicts with teachers or administrators, language barriers, or struggles outside of school that affect their ability to focus or complete work. All of these scenarios equate to a student body with diverse backgrounds.

As migrant workers or as children of migrant families, many of these students face unique barriers in school. On average, these students move with their families at least once a year for work; some move as many as eight times a year. Each move brings the frustrations and challenges of withdrawing from one school and enrolling in another, often in a different state with different standards and expectations.

HEP is also designed to capitalize on the college environment to help students achieve the HEP goals. These students live in a dormitory on campus for the duration of the 12-week program. The HEP offices are located in the same dormitory. The HEP staff that directly works with students consists of an associate director, recruiter, secretary, four instructors, and two residential mentors.

HEP participants engage in a rigorous preparation process to pass the GED exam. The four instructors provide in-depth instruction in the five GED subject areas (math, reading, writing, science, and social studies). To accommodate their comfort and confidence levels, HEP students may take their classes in either Spanish or English. In addition, students participate in a career-development course in which they prepare for career, college, or post-HEP pursuits. Twice weekly, students attend official practice test sessions that simulate actual GED testing.

Unfortunately, although the established passing rate goal for HEP was documented as 75%, the program had historically fallen short of achieving this goal prior to my joining HEP. Despite the HEP staff's commitment to student success, students had not been effectively prepared to pass the GED. To target this shortfall, MSU included many student services within the program structure to assist students with the transitional and academic issues that often become barriers to student success. However, those services had not been sufficient to increase the percentages of students passing the exam. I developed the Pedagogy of Real Talk to address that insufficiency.

## THE PEDAGOGY

A major component within the Pedagogy of Real Talk is the concept of Real Talk, an instructor-led discussion surrounding a series of broad, engaging universal themes designed to motivate student-oriented outcomes and to establish connections, understanding, trust, empathy, and caring for one another. This concept alone has utility; as the foundation of this approach, however, it is the combination with other components that makes it distinct and successful. This unique and more encompassing foundation is a combination of the theories of Paulo Freire, Margo Mastropieri and Thomas Scruggs, and Joan Meyer, along with my work with students at risk. As the core of this pedagogy, Real Talk establishes connections between teachers and students, dismantling the barriers between students at risk and teachers that inhibit the learning process. This approach is based on four main concepts: (1) relating to and connecting with students, (2) understanding students' personal perspectives, (3) creating and maintaining a flexible framework in one's teaching strategies, and (4) upholding one's willingness and eagerness to work with students. However, the ability to relate to students is a skill that is not easily taught. Only through actual face-to-face interactions with students on a consistent basis can teachers establish relatedness.

In preparing to work with the students at risk, establishing an environment of open communication from the first day is critical. In such an environment, teachers gain unique insight into students. Being an active listener allows teachers to relate better to students and to create an engaging, exciting, worthwhile classroom environment. By *active listening*, I refer to an explicit effort not only to hear the words of students but also to listen to the entire message they are trying to convey. Incorporating active listening with students can be achieved by implementing a few simple steps:

- Look at them directly; they must have your undivided attention (no multi-tasking).
- Pay attention to their body language.
- Use your body language to show them you are listening (e.g., nodding your head occasionally, smiling when appropriate, offering small comments like "uh huh" or "yes" to encourage them to continue speaking).
- Do not interrupt them as they are trying to make their point. Foster genuine communication with students, allowing them to teach you about their perspectives, realities, worldviews, and experiences.

With this information, I developed lectures, lessons, and assignments focused on their experiences. The HEP students were extremely receptive to my pedagogy because the material covered in class was directly related to their lives. However, this alone did not guarantee they would pass the GED.

I continued to refine my approach by ensuring that all class activities were inclusive and integrated the core concepts of the curriculum. The students became more engaged in class and receptive to learning. Because they needed to develop a deeper understanding of the concepts related to the GED exam, I focused on integrating those concepts into Real Talk. Providing a consistent classroom structure throughout the semester was also crucial to the students' success.

In the following chapter, I explain the Pedagogy of Real Talk more fully. We will explore the theoretical foundations of the pedagogy, learn more about the case study conducted to validate the success of this alternative methodology and the students involved in that study, see how various aspects of the pedagogy were implemented, and learn how to implement the Pedagogy of Real Talk in any classroom with any subject matter.

If you have been looking for ways to reach your students at risk, help them succeed, and find tools with which to sharpen your teaching continually, read on. The approach can be used by first-year teachers, 30-year veterans, and anyone in between. Teachers of all backgrounds, racial groups, gender, sexuality, and social classes can use this approach with any population of students at risk. The focus of this pedagogy is not the teacher or the teacher's background; it is the connections established with the students, regardless of background. It is about maximizing connections through universal emotions that are not necessarily focused specifically on life experiences alone. The Pedagogy of Real Talk will give you the framework and strategies to succeed.

# 2

---

# *Real Talk*

T eaching through methods and strategies that build better connections with students improves the academic performance of youth. That's what the Pedagogy of Real Talk is all about. The word *pedagogy* comes from the Greek roots *pais* ("child") and *ago* ("to lead"), meaning "to lead a child." In education, the term refers to specific approaches used by teachers to transmit knowledge, usually through structured curricula, to students. The pedagogy teachers choose becomes the basis for designing and implementing lessons, in-class assignments, homework, study guides, reviews, and other exercises to help their students learn the expected curriculum content. The specific approach chosen by the teacher also dictates the type of relationship created between the teacher and the student. By creating inclusive, structured, student-oriented learning environments, teachers can achieve success with their students at risk.

## THE THEORETICAL FOUNDATIONS OF REAL TALK

The Pedagogy of Real Talk is a teaching approach founded on a combination of three existing models of education, extracting concepts from the work of Paulo Freire[1] on liberation education, of Margo Mastropieri and Thomas Scruggs[2] on promoting inclusion in the classroom, and of

---

[1]Paul Freire, *Pedagogy of the Oppressed* (New York: Continuum, 1970).

[2]Margo Mastropieri and Thomas Scruggs, "Promoting Inclusion in Secondary Classrooms," *Learning Disability Quarterly* 24, no. 4 (2001): 265–274.

Joan Meyer[3] on characteristics of successful teachers. Doing so maximized the strengths of each approach because they complement each other. The work was strengthened further by the additional concepts I integrated. Thus, the Pedagogy of Real Talk encompasses more than any individual model.

In the following sections, each of the contributions from these models is further examined: dialogue (Freire), S.C.R.E.A.M. (Mastropieri and Scruggs), and the characteristics of successful teachers (Meyer).

## Dialogue

In *Pedagogy of the Oppressed*, a book dedicated to the poor of Brazil, Freire offered a major pedagogical approach for teachers to use in working with disadvantaged populations. Emphasizing the concept of dialogue, this model fosters teachers and students learning from one another. By integrating students' input and perspectives in the learning process, teachers make lessons more relevant to students' lives while encouraging them to become an intricate part of the classroom. In doing so, teachers recognize and affirm students' voices, resulting in an environment in which students and teachers grow together.

Freire focused on "the fundamental goal of dialogical teaching" in which learning and knowing "involve theorizing about experiences shared in the dialogue."[4] In this liberation education model, teachers take a role with their students in relating to their students' perspectives and lives. Rather than the traditional roles within classrooms of "teacher of the students and students of the teacher,"[5] both teachers and students are teachers and students. In Freire's terminology, they become "teacher–student with students–teachers."[6] As such, both teachers and students have responsibility for the process, allowing each person to grow.

Teachers must develop learning environments dedicated to the lives of students at risk by connecting their life experiences to learning. Teachers begin this process by learning about their students through the established dialogue. As the teachers learn about their students' lives and the things that are pertinent to them, teachers can teach in a manner that is relevant to their students' lives. Instead of using a strict approach to curriculum that is not effective with the oppressed (i.e., students at risk), teachers base lessons and lectures on the experiences and lives of their students.

---

[3]Joan Meyer, *How Teachers Can Reach the Disadvantaged: Relating to the Students, Teaching the Students, and Attitudes Towards the Students* (University Park: Pennsylvania State University, Institute of Human Resources, 1968).

[4]Donald Macedo, introduction to *Pedagogy of the Oppressed*, by Paul Freire (New York: Continuum, 2000), 17.

[5]Freire, *Pedagogy of the Oppressed*, 80.

[6]Ibid.

This dialogue is also the basis for Freire's problem-posing approach through which teachers use the reflections of their students to reform their own reflections. Through dialogue with their teachers, students become critical investigators, creating a continuous state of interaction and active listening. Thus, classrooms become places that foster critical development. As teachers pose problems related to their students and their world, they challenge students to respond. With such problems, students begin to see interrelationships within the context of the world in which they live rather than irrelevant information. With each problem, their comprehension becomes more critical.

Students at risk maintain their engagement as they learn the subjects and concepts being taught because with each new challenge, they develop new understandings. In turn, their responses lead to new challenges. Through the dialogue process, then, students feel "less alienated"[7] and become committed to learning in their classrooms. Unfortunately, many educators within the United States have adapted this pedagogy into a methodological approach rather than using the dialogue Freire intended.

## S.C.R.E.A.M.

To build inclusive classrooms and work with students at risk, Mastropieri and Scruggs[8] identified six variables teachers should include to provoke more engaged and active student involvement in the classroom and throughout the learning process. These six variables are structure (S), clarity (C), redundancy (R), enthusiasm (E), appropriate pace (A), and maximized engagement (M), collectively known as S.C.R.E.A.M. In incorporating S.C.R.E.A.M. into the Pedagogy of Real Talk, there is expansion of some sections for further clarification. Teachers should analyze their classes to determine which of the six variables they are incorporating and how effectively they are doing so. In this way, teachers can identify their classroom strengths and any areas they should develop more fully.

**Structure**. This component concerns setting up the classroom with the students. Teachers must ensure that they use appropriate curriculum and that they target students' learning styles. Students should know and understand the short- and long-term goals of the class and how their teachers can assist them in achieving these goals.

**Clarity.** Clarity is imperative to ensure that (a) students understand their teachers' expectations of their students and that (b) teachers understand

---

[7]Ibid., 81.

[8]Mastropieri and Scruggs, "Promoting Inclusion in Secondary Classrooms," 265–274.

their students' expectations of their teachers.[9] Teachers should avoid making assumptions about what students know or do not know. Incorporating this variable will greatly reduce misunderstandings and misinterpretations within classrooms.

**Redundancy.** This component concerns teachers teaching subject matter in a variety of ways and allowing students to practice concepts and subject matter in diverse ways. Redundancy includes repetition, reiteration, diverse explanations and examples, and reinforcement. This in turn allows teachers to specifically address the diverse learning styles of their students.

**Enthusiasm.** This component is essential for teachers in working with students at risk. Teachers should show their enthusiasm daily throughout each class period; but this must be done in an authentic, nonsuperficial manner. If done superficially, this population of students will notice immediately, costing teachers their credibility and the opportunity to connect with their students. Teachers must show genuine enthusiasm in presenting new material and in reviewing previously introduced material. Enthusiasm does not mean pretending to be happy; it means being fervent in teaching the material to your students. We must remain positive when teaching. When we have difficult days, as do all human beings, we must be willing to be genuine about our struggles yet remain positive toward our students' success.

**Appropriate pace.** Teachers must carefully determine the appropriate pace by considering student needs and learning as the class progresses. Teachers must constantly analyze and reflect on what is occurring in their classrooms to determine if the pace needs to be increased or decreased to maximize student learning. By employing a needs-based pace, teachers will help students feel that they can keep up with the teacher as they learn the material and increase their comfort level in the classroom.

In today's classrooms, teachers must teach toward state-imposed standards. Teachers must keep students on a pace that will allow them to address all of the standards within their subject areas. This can prove to be very difficult for some teachers. By taking the time to determine the appropriate pace for the class, teachers will be able to decipher what is slowing students down. Teachers can then address these issues and move the class at a brisker, more homogenous pace to achieve the necessary standards or goals.

**Maximized engagement.** This is the final component teachers should employ to support student engagement in classrooms at risk. In maximizing engagement, teachers make sure every student is involved at

---

[9]Hernandez, *Alternative Pedagogy: Empowering Teachers Through Real Talk.*

some level with what is occurring in their classroom. For example, to engage students in a lecture, ensure they are active listeners. Allow students to ask questions during the lecture. Ask for student input on the subject matter. Ask for help with distributing papers or with logistical matters in the classroom. In other words, allow students to become an intricate part of the classroom. By doing so, teachers give students a sense of worth and belonging because they are engaged in classroom matters on a day-to-day basis.

## Characteristics of Successful Teachers

The final piece of the theoretical foundation for Real Talk is the characteristics of successful teachers as defined by Joan Meyer.[10] She found three characteristics that determine a teacher's success with students at risk: (1) the ability to relate to students personally, (2) the ability to teach the students, and (3) the teacher's attitude toward the students. In relating to students, successful teachers incorporate student-centered approaches to their teaching and develop insight into their students. Such teachers are personally flexible and routinely engage in critical self-evaluation. In addition, they are willing to listen to their students and counsel them whenever needed. An important thing to remember is that we do not have to have the same experiences as our students to be able to relate with them. We must only be willing to attempt to connect with them. This allows us to relate to our students even when at first glance they may seem very different from us.

Successful teachers are flexible and creative. They are dynamic. They willingly go beyond the minimum efforts required and invest their energy into their students. They try new and different things to find successful approaches to improve their students' passing rates. Successful teachers approach their students as people, not just as their teachers. They encourage personal interactions with their students and show through their actions that they are "positive, accepting, and caring."[11]

Meyer's characteristics are an important aspect of my pedagogy. Teachers who have these qualities most easily adapt and successfully use the aspects combined within my approach. The Pedagogy of Real Talk is not about finding the most successful teachers or those struggling the most; it is about finding the teachers who are receptive to trying something new in the classroom. After all, the Pedagogy of Real Talk will not work if we are not willing to try it or to admit that we all have room for improvement within our lives. Meyer's characteristics within my approach give us an important step in finding new levels of success in working with students at risk.

---

[10]Meyer, *How Teachers Can Reach the Disadvantaged.*

[11]Ibid., 1.

# REFINEMENT OF THE PEDAGOGY OF REAL TALK

Combining aspects extracted from Freire's dialogue, Mastropieri and Scruggs's S.C.R.E.A.M. variables, and Meyer's characteristics of successful teachers, I developed the unique foundation of the Pedagogy of Real Talk. To these three education models, sociological theory was adopted as a lens through which teachers can better understand their students. Additionally three concepts were added to strengthen the Pedagogy of Real Talk: (1) terministic screen, (2) flexibility, and (3) Real Talk discussions.

## Symbolic Interactionism

To understand the perspectives of students, Herbert Blumer's[12] sociological theory of symbolic interactionism (S.I.) was used. Blumer based this theory on the fact that humans create and use symbols. Symbolic interactionism rests on three simple premises:

1. "Humans beings act toward things on the basis of the meaning that things have for them."[13]

2. "The meaning of such things is derived from, or arises out of, the social interaction that one has with one's fellows."[14]

3. "These meanings are handled in, and modified through, an interpretive process used by the person in dealing with the things he encounters."[15]

In other words, human beings respond, interact, and react to the meaning that things have for them; moreover, that meaning is created based on how other people respond to them regarding this meaning.

S.I. is crucial to the Pedagogy of Real Talk. Before we can begin to understand the complexities of student learning in our schools, we must first understand that we live in a society that is socially constructed. *Social construction* means "people behave on what they believe, not just what is objectively true. Thus, society is considered to be socially constructed through human interpretation."[16] Understanding this social construction

---

[12]Herbert Blumer, *Symbolic Interactionism: Perspectives and Method* (Los Angeles: University of California Press, 1969).

[13]Ibid., 2.

[14]Ibid.

[15]Ibid.

[16]M. L. Anderson and H. F. Taylor, *Sociology: The Essentials* (Belmont, CA: Thomson Higher Education, 2012), 16.

is the first step in seeing clearly that students are not merely students. They are people before they are students, people with diverse views and understandings of the society in which they live. Students at risk do not displace these views when they step into classrooms. Their perspectives permeate their classrooms. The same is true for educators. Their socially constructed views also infuse the classroom. Understanding and accepting this theoretical foundation is the first step in creating a foundation built on understanding that, in the classroom, the view of the teacher is not the only way to view the world; students also have their views and interpretations.

Students hold multiple identities within their lives, just as every single one of us does. In no particular order, I am a professor, a son, a brother, a cousin, an uncle, a board member, and so on. Although I am the same person, I play different roles within each identity I hold within my life and society. These things influence my social construction of reality. It is no different for our students. In the classroom, they are our students. Outside of the classroom but within the school boundaries, they may be jocks, gang members, thugs, "emos," or any other cultural style that is in vogue. Outside of school, they may be sons, daughters, fathers, mothers, leaders of groups, employees, and so on. Just like us, they are impacted by these identities. Once we understand this reality, we can begin the process of effectively teaching our students.

Comprehending and accepting that a teacher's reality may differ drastically from a student at risk is the first step in overcoming barriers between the two groups. For example, a teacher's reality may include owning a home and donating money to a local homeless shelter. A student at risk may have a reality wherein they have no home at all and wait in line at the local homeless shelter nightly to eat dinner. S.I. helps us understand that people who live within the same society and the same relative area may have quite different realities.

S.I. is not an applicable, tangible tool we can use in the classroom; rather, it is a perspective through which we work within our classrooms. This perspective begins before we ever enter our classrooms to teach. We must truly view and respect our students as people whose views are socially constructed. Through this view, we can begin the teaching process with open minds rather than the more traditional mindset of imposing our views as teacher onto our students at risk through the educational process. By understanding the S.I. approach at its most basic level, we can begin teaching in a transformative manner rather than in a potentially alienating or oppressive way.

By accepting the S.I. perspective, we can begin to understand how people make sense of the world. We can then create a dialogue with our students, communicating with them in a manner to which they are receptive. We can also focus on our students' school experiences, analyzing them to provide insight into how they communicate and how we interpret each other's perspectives.

## Terministic Screens

Kenneth Burke defined *terministic screen* as the way in which individuals view the world.[17] Individuals form their views, which are reflected in their perspectives, based on their group memberships and ascribed or achieved status as individuals within society. Thus, terministic screens are heavily influenced by an individual's group memberships (e.g., social class, race, gender, sexuality, education, political affiliation).

Rockler[18] described this concept as a way to deepen one's understanding of how people view the world around them. He used Burke's example of comparing terministic screens to the color filters photographers use. Each filter allows different aspects on the picture to be seen more clearly, each revealing different truths about the object or scene being depicted. Thus, something that seems factual or true when observed through one filter may reveal an entirely different understanding when viewed through a different filter.

Terministic screens also affect the vocabulary we use. We usually try to use words that reflect reality. However, our words are actually reflections of our perceptions of reality. In seeing one aspect of reality, we deflect another. Thus, one person's reality may not be the same as another person's because of our individual terministic screens. In other words, when two people see or experience the same thing, they may not perceive the experience the same way because of their filters. What may be wonderfully clear to one person can be muddled confusion to another. What one person sees as beautiful, another sees as plain, ugly, or obscene. Thus, two people in a conversation may draw very different meanings from what is said. Ultimately, terministic screens affect how we view and interpret the world.

In the Pedagogy of Real Talk, educators examine each student's terministic screen to create meaningful, relevant curriculum and learning environments, inclusive of each student's learning needs. Teachers can also understand their own perspectives better. In trying to understand their students, teachers must attempt to determine and understand their terministic screens. As a result, no longer will students simply listen to the teacher; they will also engage with their teachers in building effective pedagogy.

## Flexibility

The second concept, flexibility, is added to the S.C.R.E.A.M. variables. Flexibility is the teacher's ability to incorporate every aspect of S.C.R.E.A.M.

---

[17]Ross Winterowd, "Kenneth Burke: An Annotated Glossary of His Terministic Screen and a 'Statistical' Survey of His Major Concepts," *Rhetoric Society Quarterly* 15, no. 3–4 (1985): 145–177.

[18]Naomi R. Rockler, "Race, Whiteness, 'Lightness,' and Relevance: African American and European American Interpretations of Jump Start and The Boondocks," *Critical Studies in Media Communication* 19 (2002): 398–418.

across multiple classes with a variety of students while always maintaining the possibility for change. With flexibility, teachers can adapt core concepts to the unique needs of all students and achieve consistent results over time with different sets of students.

Too often as educators, we allow rigidity to overtake our approach to teaching, making it difficult for us to part with comfortable teaching routines. Maintaining the status quo may seem to make teaching easier, but ultimately, it does not fully benefit our students. We need to grow continually as teachers, learning new information to build a flexible repertoire of lessons, lectures, classroom assignments, and homework. With flexibility, we can foster environments inclusive of all our students' unique needs and learning characteristics.

## Real Talk Discussions

The last concept and the most powerful component of the pedagogy is Real Talk discussions. Real Talks are instructor-led discussions based on a series of broad, engaging universal themes to motivate student-oriented outcomes. Real Talk is a systematic yet authentic approach to establishing understanding, trust, empathy, and caring for one another through which teachers can establish powerful, genuine connections with their students or between their students and the established curriculum.

Universal themes can be quite diverse. For example, themes tied to experiences with happiness, anger, motivation, frustration, sadness, excitement, bitterness, or confusion can be used to generate Real Talk discussions. However, these are just examples, and no teacher should feel limited to these themes. The point of universal themes is that everyone can relate to them at some level or another. Regardless of social class, race, gender, sexuality, level of education, or unique experiences, we all have common human needs or emotions that we share. Thus, teachers should identify Real Talk themes that resonate or connect not only with themselves but also with their students.

To give a more vivid explanation of how to use Real Talk in the classroom, we must imagine a funnel. We pick a theme such as adversity and begin at the top of the funnel. If necessary, we define adversity and make sure everyone in class knows what it means. As we proceed further down the funnel, we connect adversity to ourselves (the teacher). We explain how we know adversity and how we've experienced it or how friends, family, or loved ones have experienced adversity.

The best and most powerful examples are those from our own lives or the lives of friends, family members, and loved ones. However, if we don't have any examples that are applicable to the theme or if we are uncomfortable sharing our experiences, we can pull examples from other sources, such as autobiographies, documentaries, music lyrics, or current news stories. I must stress, however, how powerful our own personal examples are.

Therefore, teachers who find it difficult to engage in Real Talk because it is uncomfortable or scary or who are unwilling to try this approach should speak with teachers who are using Real Talk successfully. Don't give up on the approach before giving it a fair chance.

After connecting the theme (i.e., adversity) with ourselves, we move further down the funnel, transitioning to our students by asking them about their experiences with adversity: How do they know adversity within their own lives? How have they experienced it? If they are shy or unwilling to discuss their personal experiences, ask them how their friends, family, or loved ones have experienced adversity. It is at this juncture that we begin to make connections with our students, allowing them to share and connect with us in the classroom. We may not get immediate jumping-out-of-seats, anxious-to-be-involved reactions during the first few Real Talks, but we will notice a change in the demeanor and atmosphere of the class. Slowly but surely, we will have one or two students raise their hands and share something regarding adversity within their lives. Those not sharing openly may be engaging in self-reflection or nodding in agreement, indicating they relate to the questions.

Continuing down the funnel, we begin to connect the Real Talk discussion to the classroom. We have multiple ways to do this. Through Real Talk, we establish and deepen our connections with students. We can also inspire, refocus, or encourage our classes. Additionally, we can use Real Talk to help our students become receptive to concepts, lessons, chapters, or anything else they must learn in class that they usually resist or find intimidating.

I once used pain as a theme and shared a negative and unfortunate experience I had had in school on Valentine's Day. I also shared how, in the long run, that experience had motivated me throughout my life. I used this specific story with my students shortly after they had experienced racial attacks at the university. I wanted to reengage them rather than lose them to the rage they were feeling as victims of racial discrimination. Through the Real Talk focused on my Valentine's Day experience, I turned the students' anger into something more productive, redirecting it to their schoolwork.

Real Talk allows us to connect with students, build rapport, and gain insight to their terministic screens. Even though the most powerful person in the classroom is the teacher, students have their own form of power: the power to resist teachers and their attempts to engage their students. Through Real Talk, we can make meaningful connections with our students, especially in classrooms where we may be having difficulty in establishing connections. Helping our students become receptive, in turn, allows us to teach them.

Real Talk also helps to dispel the common notion many students have that teachers only exist in the classroom. Students who see their teachers outside the classroom are often disbelieving, saying such things as "Mrs. Smith? What are you doing here?" when they see her at the grocery store.

It does not occur to them, as they see Mrs. Smith holding a jar of peanut butter, that she's out of food at home and, like the students or their parents, has come to the supermarket to buy groceries. Such incidents should show us that our students do not view us as people but as teachers. It's as if, when the students leave their classrooms, they believe we stand up, walk to a corner, and plug ourselves into a power outlet to recharge because the next day, our students see us in the same classroom settings we were in the day before. Real Talk helps us dismantle this idea, showing our students that we are persons before we are teachers.

This phenomenon works in reverse as well. Seeing our students outside of class can give us entirely different perspectives about who they are. Through Real Talk, we can begin to see the complex people sitting in front of us rather than merely groups of students. Thus, Real Talk is an extremely valuable tool in helping us overcome the barriers between students at risk and us, their teachers. Such barriers, which are otherwise seldom overcome, hinder the teaching and learning that is supposed to take place in our classrooms.

## Strategic Placement of Real Talk

Teachers need time and practice to become comfortable enough with Real Talk to use it effectively in their classrooms. It is not a technique that can be "winged." Practice does not mean preparing note cards as one does for formal presentations. Rather, it means feeling comfortable with engaging students in Real Talk within the classroom. This involves being authentic yet structured enough that each Real Talk discussion has a clear purpose and a point that connects with their students. As teachers become more comfortable with Real Talk and more advanced in using it within their classrooms, they will begin to recognize teachable moments in their classrooms when they can connect to a Real Talk on the spot. They will also find their students initiating Real Talks, giving teachers another avenue to contribute in a meaningful manner.

Real Talk is not something teachers should use every day. Doing so will diminish the significance of these talks. Teachers who have been trained in Real Talk and have applied it in their classrooms have constantly heard their students ask, "When will you do one of your special talks again?" We keep students on the edge of their seats by delving into strategically placed Real Talks.

Teachers should follow a general time frame in implementing Real Talks, placing them periodically throughout the duration of their courses. Strategically embedding three different Real Talk discussions over the semester is ideal. The first interaction with students is crucial to establish connections or, at the very least, a neutral setting that can lead to positive relationships. The first Real Talk can be planned for the first day of class to captivate students and "hook" them with the first interaction. Using Real

Talk on the first day to captivate our students and introduce ourselves to our classes will set the tone for the semester. However, because it takes time to feel comfortable delivering Real Talks, teachers who are not comfortable using it on the first day of class should aim for one sometime during the first week of classes.

The second Real Talk should be scheduled halfway through the course. Every teacher knows that there is a point in the middle of the semester when students exponentially begin struggling to stay focused and to do their work. Mid-semester is a crucial time. If we do not act to meet their need for reinvigoration and focus, we can lose our students. An appropriate Real Talk at this point can provide just the inspiration needed to refocus and re-energize both our students and ourselves. How we tie in Real Talks at this point is ultimately at our individual discretion, based on our students, our subject matter, and ourselves. What works in one teacher's class may not be the right Real Talk for anyone else's, but if it meets the needs of our students, it's the right Real Talk to stimulate our students' attention.

The final preplanned Real Talk of the semester should occur near the end of the course, at some point one or two weeks before final exams. Because teachers know their students well by this time, including their specific needs, they will know best when to schedule this last Real Talk. Students are often "burned out" at this point in the semester. Therefore, the purpose of this final Real Talk should be an uplifting catalyst for students to end the semester in a strong fashion, both in terms of their final exams and their overall work in the class.

Ultimately, the decision about when and how often to use Real Talks is up to each teacher. The foundational placement suggested may be sufficient for many teachers. Others may find that having Real Talks once a month or using Real Talks to introduce specific lessons, concepts, or chapters that are difficult for students to grasp will be the best way to engage their students. Some teachers may also become comfortable enough to use Real Talks sporadically when they encounter those "teachable moments," opportunities to connect with their students in terms of a particular concept or to develop rapport. However, it is essential that teachers not overuse Real Talk during a course. Overuse will diminish the power and influence of Real Talk.

## THE PEDAGOGY OF REAL TALK AND OTHER APPROACHES

In most pedagogies, teachers are expected to give the required information to students. This may be done in various ways, including lectures, videos, texts, activities, and exercises. Some pedagogies will also ask teachers to get to know their students or perhaps to understand "where their students come from" to be more effective when teaching them. Seldom, however, are teachers given a step-by-step approach on how to connect or get to know their students. Thus, in most approaches, teaching ultimately involves one-way communication: The teacher teaches; the students learn.

Real Talk is different. It is a two-way process. Not only does the teacher teach the students, but the students also teach the teacher. When teachers teach their curricula with this pedagogy, they are not using an approach that is exclusively teacher led; nor is it focused simply on filling students with the required information. This two-way teaching process is essential to the success of Real Talk.

In traditional pedagogies, teachers get to know their students mainly through structured, often inflexible processes of formal, systematic observations and ongoing assessments and documentation of learning. In Real Talk, teachers get to know their students through meaningful dialogue as well. Teachers learn about their students from their students: their lives, their perspectives, and their insights. By engaging students as people outside of their roles as students, teachers can structure their classes according to their students' needs and their abilities to relate curricular concepts to their lives. Real Talk allows teachers to establish a systematic yet authentic way to captivate and connect with their students, including their students at risk, while remaining themselves.

In most traditional pedagogies, teachers are also the solution finders. When something is not working and students are not learning as they should, the teachers are the ones with the responsibility to determine what is wrong. They must find alternatives that will ensure student learning and success. In Real Talk, teachers see their students as resources and use the students' perspectives to find answers to classroom challenges.

The Pedagogy of Real Talk is also very flexible in that it does not have to be adopted in its entirety to be used effectively. Teaching is an art form that takes time to master, a process under constant evolution, which must be considered when creating a pedagogical approach for teachers to apply in their classrooms. Many approaches expect teachers to adopt an entirely new pedagogical approach to be effective with challenging students, regardless of any success teachers may have already had with students at risk.

I acknowledge, credit, and respect the many teachers who have been or are attempting to become successful in working with students at risk. Those who are achieving success are doing many things correctly, which must be acknowledged. But everyone in society has room to improve what they do within their professions. In this specific case, all educators have room to improve their craft of teaching. For that reason, the Pedagogy of Real Talk is unique in that teachers can adapt it to meet their needs in working with students at risk. Teachers struggling to find success with students at risk will find adopting the entire approach to be ideal. Teachers already using some of the elements may begin with whatever component fits into their existing classroom structure to enhance the success they are experiencing. This approach is meant to be adaptable, encompassing, and applicable in the classroom no matter how much of it a teacher chooses to use. Whether using the entire approach or selected components to fill gaps in an already successful teaching methodology, teachers simply must be willing to try the approach to see how it can improve their success with students at risk.

I worked with a first-year European American teacher at a predominantly African American urban school. This gentleman was struggling tremendously to connect with his students. He shared that he desperately and wholeheartedly wanted to make genuine connections with his students. Although he was quite receptive to the training and was willing to try the approach, I could sense some hesitation. After a few weeks, he was finally ready to begin implementing the approach in his classroom. The first day he conducted a Real Talk that was nothing short of stellar, as his email to me after this first effort showed:

Dr. Hernandez,

I wanted to share that my first Real Talk went extremely well! About 90% of my students were absolutely engaged, nodding in agreement, and their eyes fixed on our conversation . . . the most remarkable interaction was how [receptive], respectful, and engaged they were . . . Students came up to me after class, wanted to know more updates about my demeaning experience, and a few that did not share told me that they "really got" what I was saying . . . I was willing to try your approach, but I have to be honest as I was not completely sold on the type of powerful impact you said it would have on both my students and [me] . . . I am just blown away with what I have just experienced and want to keep this momentum going . . . You have made a believer out of me regarding the impact and results of your pedagogy.

What this teacher shared is ultimately what other educators will experience when using the Pedagogy of Real Talk in their classrooms. However, the Pedagogy of Real Talk takes time. Even though this teacher had tremendous success the first time he used Real Talk in his classroom, results will vary from teacher to teacher. Successful application of this pedagogy, as with any pedagogy, does not happen in an instant; it requires time to learn to apply it correctly and consistently within the classroom. It also requires open-mindedness and a wholehearted approach.

# 3

---

## *The Students, Their Experiences, and the Academic Results*

I developed the Pedagogy of Real Talk to fulfill the need for a teaching style that I could use to help students at risk succeed in school. I wanted to create a way not only to benefit students but also to aid teachers in overcoming the struggles I had witnessed others encounter in their work with this student population. However, developing an alternative pedagogy is one thing; determining that it actually works is another!

I conducted a case study investigation within the MSU HEP program over the course of two and a half years. I connected the pieces comprising Real Talk through sociological insight to create an approach to improve students' overall experience and to improve their outcomes on standardized testing. The subjects were the students in my reading and writing preparatory courses for the GED examination.

The findings showed that this alternative pedagogy had a significant positive effect on the students: strengthening authentic relationships between the students and me, engaging students in the learning process, linking their lives to the curriculum to make it relevant to them, reducing behavioral issues in the classroom that typically inhibited the learning process for all students, and igniting an interest in education with groups of students who were seemingly disconnected from school. Through the Pedagogy of Real Talk, students' passing rates on the reading and writing portions of the GED increased, not only in comparison with past reading and writing scores but also in comparison with all the other subjects during the study. Teachers in any type of educational institution willing to use the Pedagogy of Real Talk can accomplish similar types of results.

## INCEPTION OF THE CASE STUDY

I discovered MSU HEP when a friend forwarded me an announcement for an instructor position. I applied, went through the formal interview process, and was hired. I already knew I had to create and implement an alternative pedagogy to accommodate the special learning needs of this student population at risk.

Like most teachers in the classroom, I hit the ground running and immediately began to implement my pedagogical approach in my classes. After several weeks, I was observing fantastic results with my students. I had not openly shared what composed my specific approach with anyone in the program at this point. I was simply focusing on the success of my students. But as in many other schools and programs, the administrators maintained a close watch on successes and struggles that instructors were having in the classroom. The first person to notice and approach me about the success I was having was the program recruiter.

The recruiter was the first person to connect with students. He built tremendous rapport with the HEP students, meeting their families and staying well informed about their experiences. The students spoke to him honestly and openly about what they thought of their HEP instructors, whether or not they were learning, and if they felt prepared to pass their GED exams. He gained powerful insights from the students, becoming well versed in identifying what was successful and what was not in working with these students, and tried to lend support to instructors to help them succeed with the students. However, he was not well versed in teaching and admittedly knew very little pedagogy. I respected the recruiter tremendously.

One day, during a conversation with him, I heard a sense of urgency he had not previously expressed:

> I believe you are doing something special in your classes . . . No one knows anything about how to teach this population of students, and you would be helping many others if you shared your teaching style . . . Think about what you are doing, Paul, and share your approach to teaching with others so they can help students be successful.

His words motivated me to consider conducting a formal case study to document the success of the Pedagogy of Real Talk.

A week later, the director and associate director held a staff meeting regarding research and the HEP program. They had returned from meetings with the Department of Education's Office of Migrant Education and shared that little scholarly research had been done concerning the population of students HEP served. The director encouraged us to consider doing research, gathering data on our students not just for the federal government but also for the benefit of our students. Sitting there, I decided to speak with the director and the associate director regarding my research idea.

In a private meeting, I explained the case study I wanted to conduct and asked their permission to do so. They were both excited about my ideas. The associate director even volunteered to assist. Because she was in charge of daily operations, she was the person most knowledgeable about the HEP program. With her help, I conducted my case study freely over the course of five semesters. Immediately after gaining the support and approval of the directors, I filed the Institutional Review Board application with the MSU Committee on Research Involving Human Subjects. I received approval to conduct my research a few weeks later.

## HEP STUDENT PARTICIPANTS

As part of the case study, I collected data on the students I taught as well as their test scores. I also interviewed 28 of those students to gain more insights into their lives as students. Interview questions included inquiries about me as their teacher in the classroom and the strategies I used to enhance their learning. The associate director conducted these interviews because it was more appropriate for a third party to gather information about my class from my students. I categorized the student data into four classifications: family history, personal identity, past school experiences, and reasons for dropping out.

Findings showed that students' voices were an integral part of learning about their experiences in school. Too often students' voices are lost in the educational and academic arena. If we only hear and are receptive to the voices of educators, we only know half of what is happening in our schools. Whether we agree with them or not, and even when the experiences are painful to hear, students' voices help us understand how to better serve them and improve our craft.

### Family History

Typical of the HEP population served by the MSU program, the majority of students were Latino. Their families were migrant farm workers. Although most of the students had been raised in the United States and had attended U.S. schools, the parents of only 28.5% of these students had been born in the United States. Most of the others had been born in Mexico; one student's parents had been born in Haiti. Figure 3.1 shows how long my students' parents had lived in the United States.

With the large number of foreign-born parents, language was an issue for many students. Most of them preferred to use Spanish, which was the language they used most frequently at home. Although many of their parents could speak and understand English, they still had difficulty communicating in English. This affected life not only at home but also at school. Parental contributions to academics are an important part of student success.[1] However, my students with foreign-born parents reported language barriers as the predominant issue preventing parental assistance with their schoolwork.

Also affecting these parents' ability to help their children academically was their own level of education, which ranged from no formal education to completion of the lower elementary grades to high school graduation

**Figure 3.1**    Length of Time Participants' Parents Had Lived in the United States

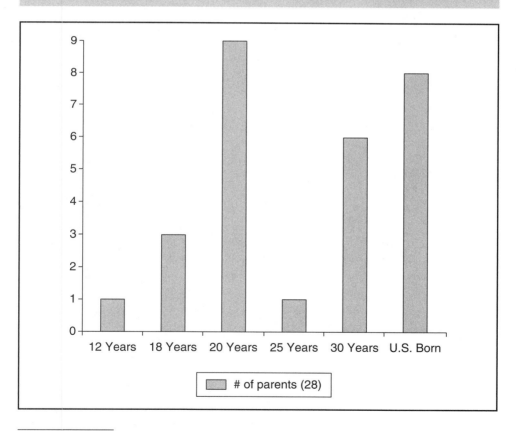

[1]Julio Antonio Pienda-Gonzales, Jose Carols Nunez, Soledad Gonzalez-Pumariega, Luis Alvarez, Cristina Roces, and Marta Garcia, "A Structural Equation Model of Parental Involvement, Motivational and Aptitudinal Characteristics, and Academic Achievement," *The Journal of Experimental Education* 70 (2002): 257–287.

(see Figure 3.2). However, 83% of my students' parents had never finished high school. Yet, despite acknowledging that their parents could not help them with their schoolwork,[2] students were not bitter or angry with their parents regarding these limitations. Lack of parental academic assistance was simply an accepted part of life.

Lack of education also negatively affected their income. Without at least a high school education, dropouts find it increasingly difficult to find work with compensation above minimum wage.[3] In analyzing the data regarding annual income, I was surprised by the diversity in the responses. The incomes reported by the 27 students responding to this question ranged from $8,000 to $45,000, with the average income being $21,888 (see Figure 3.3). However, in determining whether a family is living below the poverty level, the U.S. Department of Health and Human Services takes into consideration not only the amount of income but also the number of individuals in the household that must be supported with that income.[4]

**Figure 3.2**  Educational Level of Participants' Parents

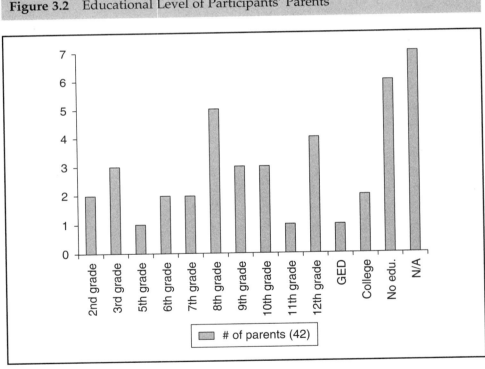

---

[2]Sook-Jung Lee and Natasha K. Bowen, "Parent Involvement, Cultural Capital, and the Achievement Gap Among Elementary School Children," *American Educational Research Journal* 43 (2006): 193–218.

[3]Hernandez, *Alternative Pedagogy: Empowering Teachers Through Real Talk*, 50.

[4]Kathleen Sebelius, "Annual Update of the HHS Poverty Guidelines," *Federal Registry* 78 (2013): 5182–5183.

**Figure 3.3**  Total Income of Participants' Households

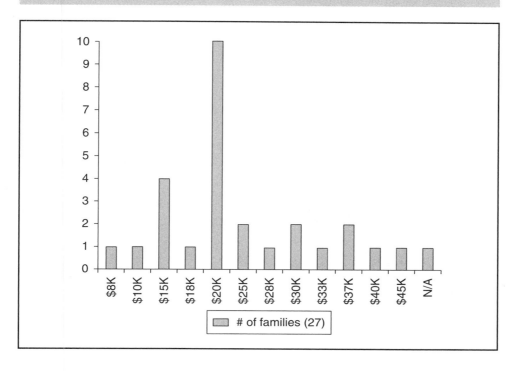

The number of people in the participants' households ranged from three to nine people, with an average of five people per household. Based on federal guidelines, 21 of the participants' families were living in poverty; however, the six families classified as being above the poverty level exceeded that level by an average of only $4,346. One student's family earned only $470 above the poverty level. Therefore, regardless of the federal guidelines, I considered all the participants' households to be living in poverty.

Single-mother households are also common in poor minority communities, a trend reflected clearly by the HEP students in the case study. Eleven (39.2%) of the students in the case study lived in families headed by single mothers. Single-parent households headed by mothers are the poorest of all types of family groups.[5] Children from these homes often perform poorly in school and exhibit more behavioral problems than children from other types of family groups. These characteristics may be attributed to the lack of time these mothers have for their children. Because of the responsibilities they must bear as heads of households, they have little time for involvement in their children's school endeavors.

---

[5]Pauline Erera, *Family Diversity: Continuity and Change in the Contemporary Family* (Thousand Oaks, CA: Sage, 2002).

## Personal Identity

All of the participants revealed a common theme of struggling in school because of experiences with personal discrimination based on their identities, both who they considered themselves to be and who others perceived them to be. In identifying themselves, students provided both basic demographic information and deeper information about how they saw themselves that helped further the understanding of their struggles.

The students ranged in age from 18 to 29 years old, with an average age of 19 years (see Figure 3.4). This was typical of the overall HEP student population. At MSU HEP, it was not unusual to have students in their 30s and 40s. Even some students in their 60s were peers of much younger students in the HEP classrooms.

The participants had been born in a variety of places (see Figure 3.5). Most were from Michigan (31.3%) and Texas (25%). Others came from Illinois (15.6%), Mexico (12.5%), California (9.4%), and Florida (6.2%). All but five of the students were raised where they were born. One student born in Michigan had been raised in Illinois, and four students born in Mexico had been raised in the United States. For that reason, the four students born in Mexico were counted twice: once for location of birth and

**Figure 3.4**   Ages of Interviewed Students

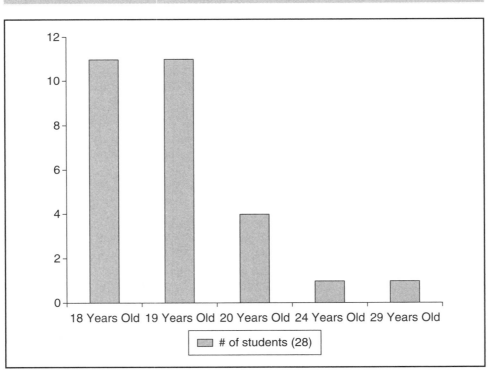

**Figure 3.5**  Where Students Were Born and Raised

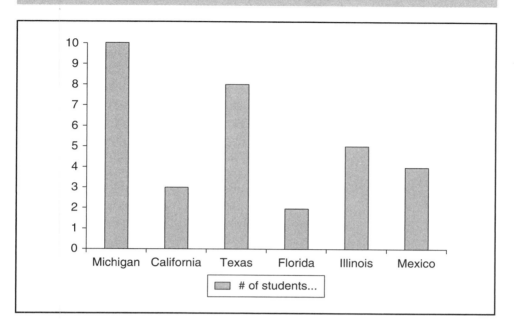

once for where they were raised. These locations identified where students developed the foundations of their self-identities.

When I first met the HEP students, I realized that many had a style of dress, vernacular, and overall demeanor that was very familiar. It was the style of thugs and gang members. I had lived my entire youth engulfed in the street gang and thug lifestyle. However, not all of my students fit into that category. Based on the descriptions provided by the students, I identified six descriptors that were indicative of these students' self-identities: thug, gang member, drug addict, gay, party girl, or normal (see Figure 3.6). Twelve (42.8%) of the participants stated they were thugs. Eight (28.5%) described themselves as gang members. Only three (10.7%) identified as normal. The self-identities of these students permeated the manner in which they navigated the education system, affecting their academic progress.

Although in other settings or with different groups, the designations of gang member and thug may mean the same thing, this group of students defined the terms differently. Compared to gang members, thugs do not formally belong to any group or gang. They are often, however, involved in many activities associated with gang members: drugs, drug dealing, theft, and vandalism. Thugs also exude an overall attitude of not caring about anyone.

The interviewed students shared that they exhibited certain poor behaviors because they were being true to the Latino identity they had created for themselves. An abundance of research exists on the concept and

**Figure 3.6**   Self-Identities of Students

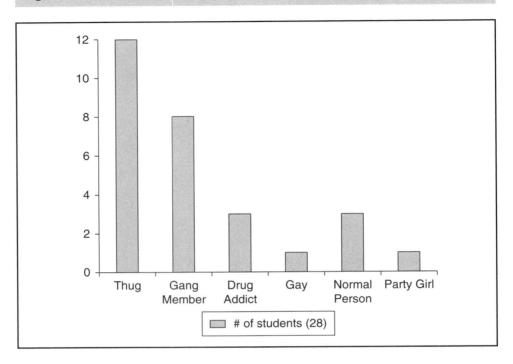

negative consequences of "acting Black" or, more appropriately in the case of these HEP students, "acting Latino."[6] *Acting Latino* is the process of taking an oppositional stance to school success, a rejection of "acting White." Among others, the perceptions many students had of acting White included being successful in school by attending classes, doing homework, paying attention in class, obeying the teacher, and participating in class activities. They rejected these behaviors because they did not want to be stigmatized as acting White, which usually resulted in being disrespected or looked down on by their peers. The rejection of such behaviors is highly correlated with low grades and overall academic failure.

Countless negative experiences and interactions during school also affected these students' self-identities. Many of these experiences were based on different forms of discrimination. Students felt stigmatized and marginalized by teachers based on their race, socioeconomic status, gang involvement, and other factors that excluded them from the norms of the

---

[6]See Sonja Lewis-Peterson and Lisa M. Bratton, "Perceptions of 'Acting Black' Among African American Teens: Implications of Racial Dramaturgy for Academic and Social Achievement," *The Urban Review* 36 (2004): 81–100; John Ogbu and Herbert Simmons, "Voluntary and Involuntary Minorities: A Cultural-Ecological Theory of School Performance with Some Implications for Education," *Anthropology and Education Quarterly* 29 (1998): 155–188.

educational system. Their feelings ultimately exacerbated their involvement with activities that further hindered their academic success, creating a vicious cycle of failure.

The effects of discrimination and its overtly negative consequences were most clearly stated and felt by students who identified themselves as thugs or gang members. One student stated,

> The way I dress, the way I talk, my tattoos, and the kind of shit I was involved with made me an easy target at school for teachers and administrators to know I am a gang member. But it is fucked up because I wouldn't do shit in school because I didn't want any drama in school, but I felt and was treated like a moving target by teachers and administrators.

This student had been targeted as a troublemaker even when he was not involved in any issues at school. Many of the case study participants shared similar sentiments.

These students also felt that being identified as a thug or gang member prevented their teachers from looking for the causes for their behaviors and for ways to remedy them. Instead, in the students' experiences, teachers tended to lump all students who identified as gang members or thugs into the same category: They were detriments to the academic process. Their teachers had made no attempts to determine or understand these students' individual circumstances that had resulted in their behaviors. Their teachers did not understand that the students' choice to associate in gang-related activities was not synonymous with a lack of educational desire. The majority of the students reported that their involvement in gang activities stemmed from the impoverished situations they experienced at home. These students became involved with drug dealing, both inside and outside of school, to survive economically and to help sustain their families. As Papachristos stated, "Gangs that do sell drugs essentially fill a void in the postindustrial urban [or rural] economy, replacing the manufacturing and unskilled labor jobs that traditionally served as a means for social mobility."[7]

## Past School Experiences

All 28 students interviewed stated they were identified as students at risk while they were in school. All 28 also felt stigmatized by that label, regardless of the reasons behind it. By categorizing all students at risk together, teachers overlook the reasons for each individual's risk. Unfortunately, for these 28 students, the stigma affected their performance

---

[7]Andrew V. Papachristos, "Gang World," *Carnegie Endowment for International Peace* 147 (2005): 50.

in school and their perceptions of their teachers and schools. Ultimately, they became part of the national dropout epidemic.

Every interviewed student had negative perceptions of either teachers or their schools. Common in their comments was the theme of boredom:

- "School was boring and I never had anything to do when I was there so I didn't like it."
- "I was tired of school because the teachers were boring and I wasn't learning anything in the classes."
- "You know, I wanted to make class interesting 'cause that shit was boring as hell! . . . Everything the teacher said was so boring."
- "There was nothing in class that was interesting and that was relevant to my life."

Dry, boring material with little or no relevance to students' lives made coming to class painful for these students.

Beyond ineffective pedagogies experienced by HEP students, discrimination was a common theme that negatively affected the students' perspectives on school. One student said, "These fucking teachers treated me and my friends like shit compared to how they treated the upper class White kids in school." Another said, "A teacher called me a loser." A third stated,

In my school the teachers and students discriminated against me a lot because I was a farm worker. The students called me racist names and were real mean to me. Teachers treated me like I was stupid because I worked in the fields, and they didn't do anything about the other students calling me racist names.

Teachers control the arena of the classroom, an intensely personal environment. Teacher–student relationships affect students' grades and overall success.[8] Thus, having teachers listen and find ways to help students is extremely important. However, the participants in this case study seldom experienced such relationships, as one student said:

I never went to school because I had problems with gangs in school. Teachers didn't care about what I would tell them I was dealing with. I mean I pretty much asked them for help or some advice on what I could do, and they would just ignore me or say they couldn't help me. They didn't give a fuck about me or my life.

---

[8]Travis L. Gosa and Karl Alexander, "Family (Dis)Advantage and the Educational Prospects of Better Off African American Youth: How Race Still Matters," *Teachers College Record* 109 (2007): 285–321.

Another student expressed that teachers simply "did not get it":

Teachers didn't know what was going on in the "real world" with all the shit I had to deal with. I mean I really fucking hated teachers because they just didn't get it and still wanted me to do what they wanted. They also hated me 'cause I was Mexican, and I wasn't stupid and knew they were racist by how they treated me.

Given the number of negative experiences shared by so many of the HEP students, I clearly understood why they had formulated negative perspectives of schools and teachers.

Disciplinary issues were also a problem for these students at risk. For the purposes of this case study, *disciplinary issues* were defined as those behaviors, either in class or outside class but on school premises, that resulted in some kind of disciplinary action being taken against them. Such actions included office referrals, parental contacts, detentions, in-house suspensions, and suspensions. The majority of the interviewed students (61%) encountered disciplinary issues inside the classroom (see Figure 3.7). A smaller group (21%) received disciplinary actions for behavior both in class and outside class.[9] The high percentage of referrals within the classroom evidenced constant conflict between teacher and student in the classroom.

Although HEP students were generally understood to be troublemakers in school, disciplinary issues were more complex. In discussing the reasons for their involvement in disciplinary issues, the students revealed they had very different perspectives than their teachers concerning the situations and their punishments. One student expressed that his teachers would not listen to him: "They would never hear me out . . . I didn't agree with the things teachers would say so I would challenge them and ask questions, but they would treat me like I was crazy." This student particularly challenged his teachers regarding history and the information being taught that he thought was biased. He felt teachers ignored history that was not European American in orientation, a view supported by research.[10] Rather than embrace his unique, controversial perspective and use it in a constructive manner to aid class learning, teachers met this student's perspectives with disdain, making him feel ostracized. Many of the student participants felt similarly, that teachers either lacked understanding or were unwilling to understand. Therefore, these students experienced a general lack of respect by their teachers, which resulted in many of the

---

[9]Hernandez, *Alternative Pedagogy: Empowering Teachers Through Real Talk*, 68.

[10]See Gary Nash and Julie Roy Jeffrey, eds., *The American People: Creating a Nation and a Society* (New York: Longman, 2001); Howard Zinn, *A People's History of the United States: 1492–Present.* (New York: Harper Perennial, 1995).

**Figure 3.7**   Disciplinary Issues by Location

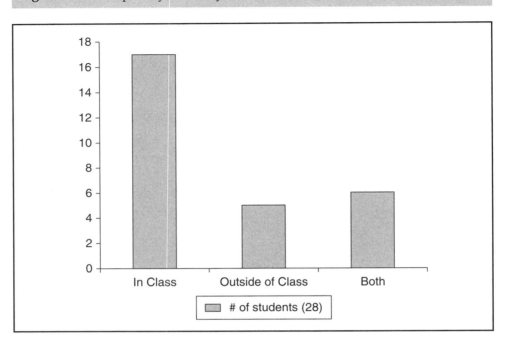

behavioral issues that pitted teacher against student. The HEP students also felt that they were disciplined more readily and severely than their European American counterparts.

The majority of the student participants (82%) were involved in disciplinary issues within the classroom that hindered their academic performance; however, 18% were involved in disciplinary issues outside the classroom. One student was constantly in trouble due to drug use. Her frustration increased, however, because she felt that her teachers did not care: "They say they cared and would help us if we had any problems, but they never helped me with my issues." She had not expected teachers to solve her drug problem, but she had hoped that they would serve as a resource to find help.

Another participant also found that his teachers were not useful resources when he needed help. He had been constantly involved in fights at school with members of rival gangs. He had tried to approach his teachers to make them aware of the issues he faced and to explain why he was involved in so many fights. He had hoped for advice, referrals to resources for help, or even understanding of the issues. Instead, he had met with unresponsive, nonempathetic teachers:

> When I would go to school, I would get into all kinds of fights because of my enemies going to the same school. The teachers did not care about the drama that would go down as long as it did not

happen in class. So they were happy whenever I would not go to class because whenever I would show up, they thought something was going to go down. I tried talking to them about what the problems were, but they always told me that I needed to take care of these things outside of school property and to not bring my problems to school.

Another student stated,

I just hated school. I also had to deal with a lot of drama with people talking shit because I am gay. I wouldn't just let people talk shit, so I would call people out and fight because I was not going to let anyone talk shit about me. The teachers didn't do anything about punishing the people who would talk shit to me, so I would handle it myself.

## Reasons for Dropping Out

Although many of the reasons these students dropped out of school are apparent in the previous sections, 60.7% of these students had managed to stay in school until sometime during the 11th grade. One had even begun senior year. Therefore, understanding what the "last straw" had been for these students was imperative to understanding their situations. The students' responses revealed two categories of reasons (see Figure 3.8): (1) the school itself and (2) personal or financial reasons. Because the financial reasons were often personal in nature, these two kinds of reasons were combined into one category.

Of the 28 students interviewed, 16 (57%) dropped out of school because of the school itself, which included teachers, administrators, and general negative experiences. Many of the students dropped out of school because of their negative interactions with teachers. One student clearly expressed the power of teachers' words over those of their students:

I ended up dropping out in the 11th grade because I was kicked out. I was kicked out because of a fucking teacher. The fucking guy claimed that I threatened to kill him. He said he read my lips and he knew I said I would kill him.

Years later, this student told me, "Man, Paul, I have no reason to lie about it. I never told that teacher I would kill him, but they believed him and not me." Another student also told about his experience with the power of teachers:

I ended up dropping out because of an argument I got into with a teacher. A teacher called me a loser and I flipped out and started cursing and going crazy on the teacher because of what he told me.

Because of how I acted, no one believed me that he called me a loser; and it turned into how I acted instead of what the teacher did to start the whole thing.

A third student suffered a comparable fate:

I dropped out in the 10th grade because of a huge riot they say I started. There was this White guy who was a senior and was a big time racist. He would call all of us Latinos Spics, dirty Mexicans, Beaners, and all kinds of racist shit. Well, I got tired of his shit and called him out after school one day. All the Latinos in the school were tired of his shit cause this motherfucker tried terrorizing us and the school didn't do shit. So I decided to do something about it, and he met me after school to fight. News spread around school real quick, and I didn't even know what was going to happen because I was planning to kick this guy's ass one-on-one style. When we met up after school, I was surprised when I saw about 50 Latino students show up to confront this guy; and before you know it a huge riot broke out. This guy got hurt real bad and shit went down; but at the end of the day, it all fell on me. The school held me responsible and I was kicked out. I never went back because I felt that it wasn't fair because I was just standing up for myself because no one else would. But the school didn't give a fuck so I just stopped going.

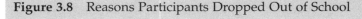

**Figure 3.8**   Reasons Participants Dropped Out of School

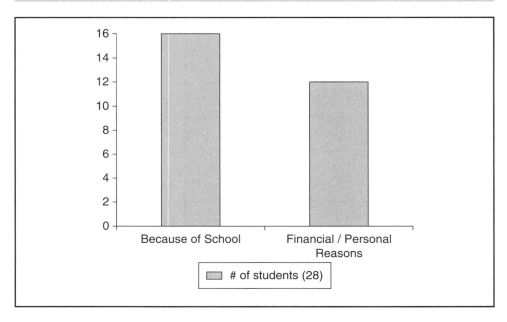

Falling victim to racism, this student had felt cornered and responded in the manner he had felt was best because the authority figures in school had taken no action. In fact, the school never took action against this student's agitator, resulting in the participant's decision to drop out.

A fourth student shared a different form of teacher influence, although it ended with the same result:

> Teachers were always rude and mean to me and were always judging me. I fell too far behind in my schoolwork, and a teacher told me I would never graduate; so I decided to drop out after she told me that in the 11th grade.

Teacher influence has been well documented.[11] In the case of these HEP students, this influence was clearly a factor in their decision not to complete their education.

The remaining 12 students (43%) identified either personal or financial reasons for dropping out. Students who dropped out for financial reasons stated that they needed money for survival. Although many of these students also experienced similar negative situations as the students who dropped out because of the school itself, those experiences were not the primary reason they left school, as one student stated:

> I mean, me and my family was starving and we needed money; and teachers didn't give a fuck. So I ended up dropping out in the 11th grade because I needed to make steady money for my family. I didn't care about school though, Paul. I just hated that fucking place 'cause the teachers always tried to make me feel stupid.

Getting married, gang problems, legal issues outside of school, and general personal problems not directly connected to school were all identified as personal reasons for dropping out. One student stated that he "decided to get married and go to work so I could support myself and my wife instead of wasting my time in a place (school) that I hated." These students were disconnected from school and did not see how it related to their lives. They did not see a value in education; other things in life had more value than school. Other students declared that drugs and problems with gangs were the predominate issues that influenced their decision to drop out.

Regardless of the reasons these students cited for dropping out of school, they were each negatively affected by the decision to do so. For example, it was common for some students to discuss how they were "stuck in the same dead-end" jobs that they had begun working after

---

[11]See Valeria Lee and David T. Burkham, "Dropping Out of High School: The Role of School Organization and Structure," *American Educational Research Journal* 40 (2003): 353–393.

dropping out of school. Every student interviewed took responsibility for that decision. However, each student's background served as a starting point in understanding the reasons they had not succeeded in traditional school systems in which teachers employed traditional pedagogical approaches.

## THE RESULTS

Implementing the Pedagogy of Real Talk helped HEP students pass the reading and writing sections of the GED with increased rates. Students not only achieved significant increases in passing rates but were also more engaged while in class, decreasing classroom misbehavior. Off-topic, personal conversations during class decreased. Daydreaming or sleeping became nonexistent as students grew more eager to participate in lessons and discussions. Assignment completion rates increased because the students felt personally connected with the topics. They wanted to offer their experiences and insights because they could see their offerings were valued and incorporated into the curriculum. With decreased disciplinary issues, lessons became easier to set up, students' willingness to engage in learning increased, and teaching became easier. Thus, rather than spending a large portion of time managing the class or disciplining students, more attention could be focused with students in the specific skill areas in which they needed the most assistance.

Specifically, students posted significant increases compared with the classes taught by the previous instructor from the very first semester I employed my alternative pedagogy. Figure 3.9 shows the passing rates in reading for the previous instructor's six semesters and the rates for the five semesters I taught as part of the case study. Over the course of those five semesters, students averaged a 97.2% passing rate in reading. Two of the semesters, students achieved 100% passing rates.

In the writing portion of the GED examination, students also significantly exceeded the passing rates of the previous instructor's classes (see Figure 3.10). According to the HEP administrators and staff, writing and math were typically the most difficult subjects for HEP students. Over the course of the five semesters, students had an average passing rate of 94.6%; and in the last semester of the case study, 100% of students passed the writing portion of the exam. Thus, in both the reading and writing classes, students exceeded the HEP program goal of 75% passing rates.

In the fall semester of year two, a second set of reading and writing classes were added to the HEP program. These classes, taught in Spanish, were established to meet the needs of the migrant community and to prepare students to take the GED examination in Spanish. The Spanish-language classes mirrored the English-language classes. HEP students could choose which language they wished for both instruction and testing.

**Figure 3.9**   Passing Rate Comparison of Reading Classes: Former Instructor
(FY1–SY3) and Paul (FY4–FY6)

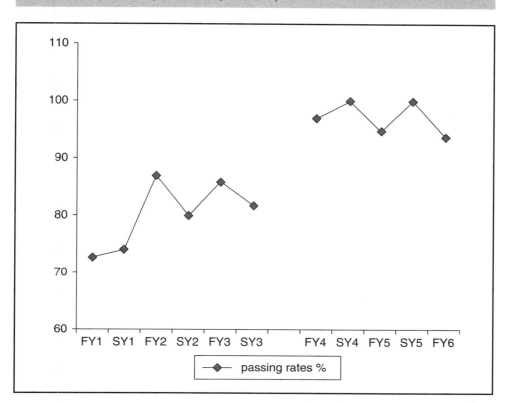

Being separated for instruction in their preferred languages did not carry the stigma associated with being assigned to ESL/ELL classes or tracked curricula in traditional schools. Therefore, the students remained united as a group. Personal choice was the deciding factor.

Figures 3.11 and 3.12 show comparisons of the passing rates for the reading and writing portions of the GED for my classes and for the Spanish language classes. The difference between the two is quite clear: Students in the case study scored up to 40% higher than the students in the Spanish-language sections.

Through this alternative pedagogy, I was also able to provide other teachers with methods to help them connect and build rapport with their students. In the fall of year three, I worked closely with a new instructor who was taking over the Spanish language reading and writing classes. She applied the alternative pedagogy with relative ease and significantly increased the passing rates for her students at the end of the Fall year three semester (see Figures 3.11 and 3.12). Another instructor who implemented the approach and yielded similar performance results solidified the success of the Pedagogy of Real Talk and its applicability to other instructors.

**Figure 3.10**    Passing Rate Comparison of Writing Classes: Former Instructor (FY1–SY3) and Paul (FY4–FY6)

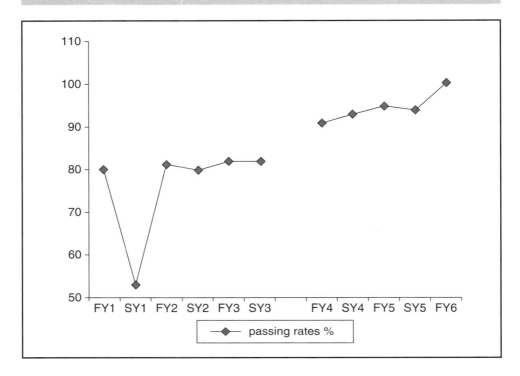

**Figure 3.11**    Passing Rate Comparison of Reading Classes in English (Paul) and Spanish

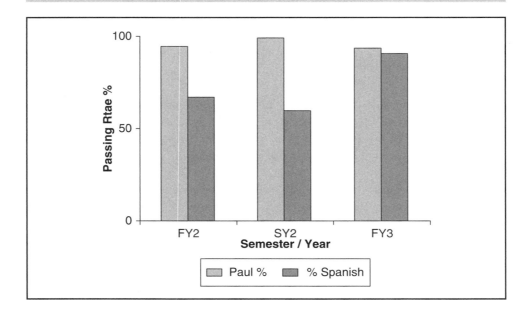

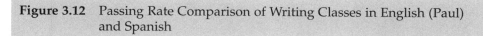

**Figure 3.12**   Passing Rate Comparison of Writing Classes in English (Paul) and Spanish

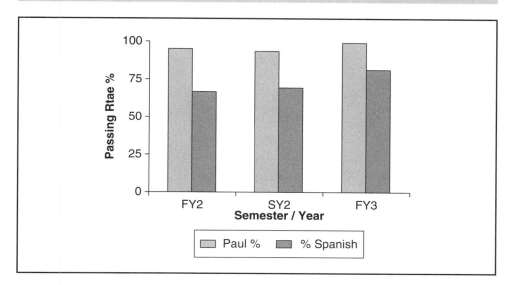

Additional support for this alternative pedagogy can be seen in comparing the results from my reading and writing classes to the results in the other three GED subject areas: science, social studies, and math. As shown in Figure 3.13, students' performance in those three areas was consistently lower compared with their performance in reading and writing.

**Figure 3.13** Overall Student Performance in All Subject Areas During Study Period

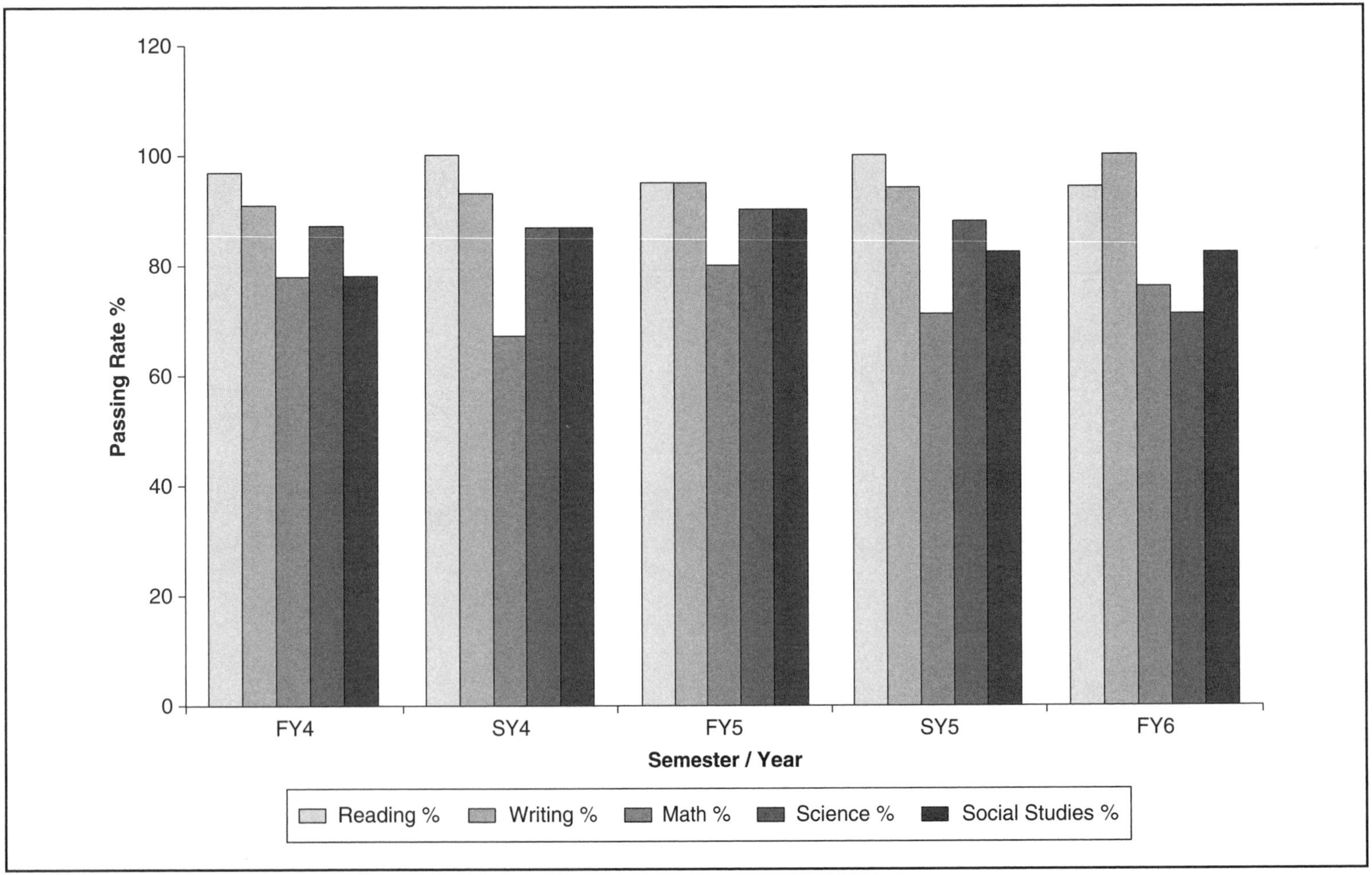

# 4

## *Implementing Real Talk in the HEP Program*

I n Chapter 2, the foundations of the Pedagogy of Real Talk were
discussed: dialogue based on Freire's *Pedagogy of the Oppressed*,
S.C.R.E.A.M., Meyer's characteristics of successful teachers, terministic
screens, flexibility, and Real Talk discussions. However, knowing what the
pieces are and knowing how to put them all together are not the same. Just
as we need to see the picture of the completed puzzle to put the individual
pieces in the right positions, so too do we need to understand the overall
purpose and components of a pedagogy before we can put them together
to help students achieve academic success.

In the next three chapters, we will look at the details of the implementation of the Pedagogy of Real Talk. This chapter details the implementation
of dialogue relating to students, structure, clarity, redundancy, enthusiasm,
appropriate pace, and maximized engagement. Chapter 5 discusses flexibility, adaptability, and effort. The most powerful component, Real Talk
discussions, is the topic of Chapter 6. Because some of the concepts within
the pieces are similar, determining if something in the implementation of
the pedagogy is an example of flexibility or adaptability, for example, is
moot. I've combined such concepts in these chapters to give a true por-
trayal of how the Pedagogy of Real Talk was implemented in classrooms.

In addition, as with any pedagogy, implementation was an ongoing
process. As you gain a better understanding of the Pedagogy of Real Talk,

you will refine your skill in implementing the components. With each semester, you will establish connections with your students faster. This is crucial in the arena of education because we do not have the luxury of time.

# DIALOGUE

Dialogue is embedded throughout the Pedagogy of Real Talk. It cannot really be separated from all of the other components because it is contained within each to some extent. Thus, dialogue flows throughout the structure of class over the course of the semester.

Respect is a baseline objective in the pedagogy. The focus of class is to get to know students thoroughly to maximize their engagement in the learning process. To accomplish this, you must treat and respect students as human beings yet always maintain your professional position as the teacher. Never try to control or force students to learn. Rather, include and integrate them as part of their own learning experiences. As you and the students develop mutual levels of respect, they will feel that your desire to hear their opinions and understand their backgrounds is genuine. This, in turn, will lead to drastic increases in their interest in learning. Teachers of any background can use mutual respect as a starting point for their instructional focus.

During the first week of class with the students, I did not overwhelm them with work or assignments. Instead, we began with dialogue in the classroom. On the first day, I introduced myself as a person: my background, where I was from, and my interests outside of the classroom. After my initial introduction, I turned the floor over to the students and asked them to tell me where they were from and a bit about their backgrounds and interests outside of class. Instead of focusing on school, we began establishing a mutual dialogue in the classroom. As more and more students spoke up, I eventually transitioned our discussion to school and the purpose it serves within our lives.

I usually led the dialogue in the beginning stages of class to build trust and student confidence. I began by first giving them insights into my life and connecting it to the classroom we shared. I explained that education was something that had allowed me to take myself from the gutters of Los Angeles to the faculty offices of a Midwestern university. I explained that all the classes I had ever taken had never suggested incorporating my life experiences into the classroom, so our classroom would be different. There, everyone's stories would be used to make sense of why we were learning the things we needed to know to pass the reading and writing components of the GED.

Slowly but surely during the first week of class, more and more students shared about their lives and what education meant to them. The dialogue introduced the students' lives into the classroom, as well as mine, as we began to learn from one another. I integrated the problems into what they learned to add relevance to their learning. Ultimately, I introduced the "real world" into the often mundane world of the classroom.

I was open with my students, acknowledging the information I continually learned from them and often thanking them for teaching me something new. I was never the "all-knowing" teacher. Instead, I was their teacher who knew some things but not all things. Their excitement in knowing they taught me as much as I taught them created an electric atmosphere in which the students and I engaged in learning during the time we spent in the classroom. Thus, dialogue impacted the students in a manner that made them react positively in class. Although I gained some insights into their terministic screens and lives—Real Talk served as the most powerful approach to gain in-depth understandings of these things—I empowered them to become part of the teaching process during class.

## RELATING TO STUDENTS

Befriending students is not the intent or the focus of this approach. In the Pedagogy of Real Talk, the aim is to find ways to relate the curriculum to the students' terministic screens or experiences. The HEP associate director had strongly emphasized connecting with our students to generate success in the classroom, stating in one of our first meetings, "If you cannot connect with these students, then you will not be successful with them." The recruiter had reinforced this message. Thus, relating to my students could not be merely a matter of having some similarities with them. It had to be derived through developing rapport with them by "talking with them, laughing with them, counseling them, [and] reaching them on their own level."[1]

The associate director of HEP told me that one of the biggest issues teachers faced was relating to their students and finding ways to connect the material in meaningful ways to their lives: "I can't stress it enough. You must find a way to relate with students in order to connect with them. Once you connect, you will see; they will want to learn." Her urgency and sincerity were apparent when we spoke, but I noted that it was up to each instructor to discover the methods needed to make learning meaningful for his or her students.

The recruiter also routinely engaged me in conversations regarding students. As he prepared me for my first semester, he echoed the now familiar message:

> Paul, you must connect with them because if you do not, they will not be receptive to you or what you are trying to teach them . . . I wish I could tell you how to do it, but I can't. It will be a difficult task and I pray to God that you will find a way and be successful with all of our students. Other teachers have managed to find connections with students, so I have faith that you can too.

---

[1]Meyer, *How Teachers Can Reach the Disadvantaged*, 3.

However, it is a daunting task to identify ways to connect with students or to relate to them before even meeting them. At times, I felt overwhelmed, privately admitting feelings of defeat after discussions with colleagues regarding our students.

I typically discovered the students' personal issues and made connections during class discussions. I then used that information as a tool to create recognizable links to the curriculum. Rather than hinder or discourage discussion of these issues, I used them as teachable moments, as one of my students described during the interviews:

> His class connects with us, and I just feel like he really understands my pain and helps me learn from it. He has been there before in our shoes, and he has made it out of the gutter. He knows how to take his past and my past experiences and turn them into some real ass lessons in the classroom.

Although my students and I were very different and had not shared the exact same experiences, I emphasized engaging my students in open dialogue and, as a result, learned things about them. As I learned about them, I could see how our lives paralleled in so many ways. It was not about having the exact same experiences when it came to relating to my students; rather, it was understanding that as human beings, we share common struggles. We may experience them in different ways, but we constantly seek out ways to move onward and upward. Relating to my students was not about changing who I was or attempting to be more like them. Rather, it was about tearing down the social constructions that kept us apart. Relating to my students required a combination of willingness, transparency, eagerness, honesty, and authenticity while maintaining my position as their guide (teacher) to overcome the obstacles (GED subjects) they faced. As they recognized these things within my approach to working with them, we began to relate to each other in a meaningful manner. Ultimately, Real Talk and the other components of the pedagogy facilitated my relating to my students by making it much easier and systematic yet allowing me to remain authentic.

## STRUCTURE

Structure for my classes was based on two things: the general structure of the HEP program and the S.C.R.E.A.M. variables. Structure for students came by way of class schedules, which provided a level of consistency that many of them were not accustomed to within their personal lives. Within the HEP program, they attended classes following consistent daily and weekly schedules that they could rely on, day in and day out. They could also count on their same group of teachers being there for them throughout the entire semester. The classroom structure I created also gave them an opportunity to escape the volatility and lack of clear expectations many of my students encountered in their everyday lives.

The curriculum for the GED classes was based on the Steck-Vaughn GED textbook series and, thus, remained virtually the same each semester. This series provided students with clear expectations for coursework structure and style. Although individual teachers added supplemental materials and activities to their classes, the foundation of the curriculum remained consistent across all subjects.

In addition to the schedule and materials used, I established structure within my class by creating basic routines. During the first five to 10 minutes of every class, we discussed what was happening in my students' lives and in my life (always using discretion). Students became accustomed to having time for personal talk at the beginning of every class before delving into our work. This routine served a very powerful purpose: It removed the stress of being in a classroom by allowing students to "get things off their chests." Sometimes we smiled and laughed; on other occasions, we simply took time to know one another beyond our classroom roles. Thus, the classroom became a far less stressful place for my students. When the time allotted for these personal discussions ended, I always turned our attention back to the curriculum for the day. The small amount of time dedicated to speaking before we began working paid large dividends because the students were more focused on their schoolwork for the remainder of the class.

Another routine in my class structure was the writing of a paper every Monday. Weekends were when HEP students, like so many other students, simply forgot about school. To collect any work from them or to have them engage in work on Mondays was typically a challenging task. However, because the students were typically excited to share their weekend endeavors, I used that effectively to get them to write, creating Monday papers. These were papers students wrote about what they had done over the weekend. They knew my expectation was for them to have their papers written for the start of class on Monday. Many of these students were scared of writing and struggled to write even a paragraph. By having them tell me about their weekends, I broke through their fear of writing and slowly but surely taught them the rules they needed to become better, more competent writers. They also appreciated the fact that I read their papers and at times spoke to them or asked them questions about the things they wrote. Because they felt valued in class, over time, they wrote more and more as they became comfortable with the writing process. Just as they shared their weekends with me, I, in turn, shared mine with them, using discretion at all times. The students felt it was only fair that I do so because they were sharing with me.

Teachers can structure their classes in a variety of ways. The key is to be consistent and to allow student feedback. Once we establish routines in our classrooms, our students will regard them as classroom norms. Such norms minimize the need for constant reminders about what they need to do and reduce the occasions on which students tell us that they forgot their homework assignments. When we incorporate our students into the structure of our classrooms, they are more likely to accept what we expect of them, diminishing their level of resistance and increasing consistency in the classroom.

## CLARITY

Clarity is an important aspect of any classroom. Students echo how important it is for them to understand the material, understand me, and know my expectations of them. Thus, usage and vocabulary are important dimensions of clarity. Seldom use complex language or vocabulary in class. When you do, take the time to teach the meaning and proper use of the language you use. Therefore, you will use a combination of the students' vernacular and yours during your discussions in class, establishing a linguistic middle ground to ensure clarity.

Clarity also involves being honest with students about who you are not only as an instructor but also as a person. For example, when I found myself missing Los Angeles, I shared with my students that I was having a bad day because I felt homesick and might not be as engaging as I usually was. At times, my honesty with my students surprised my colleagues, who felt I was too open about myself. However, through this openness, I began developing relationships with my students. Those relationships stimulated students' engagement in their learning. Because of my sharing of myself, my students felt more connected, wanted to listen, and shared more about themselves and their experiences during our discussions in class.

Of more importance, clarity includes making sure students understand your expectations of them in class. Especially focus on getting students to understand that their actions have consequences and that the people around them throughout their lives, including school, may respond to their actions in different ways. Many students are not accustomed to taking responsibility for their actions, even in situations when they clearly committed inappropriate acts or broke rules or laws. In many cases, it is because they have been routinely treated unfairly or falsely accused of things both in school and in their personal lives, making it difficult to admit to anything.

Instead, they learn to obfuscate their actions and blame others, and have developed expert-level tactics to deflect responsibility, all to protect themselves. Because many students at risk expect to be disrespected and blamed, they take a defensive or standoffish stance toward educators. What has become a survival mechanism for these students ultimately works against them in the classroom. Even when they are approached by well-intentioned teachers who have the students' best interests in mind, students at risk tend to be defensive. Therefore, establishing clarity was a crucial component in breaking the defense tactics the HEP students used in the classroom.

Many HEP students, like many other students at risk, also tended to view teachers and administrators as people who disciplined them unfairly. Although some teachers and administrators did unfairly target students at risk, assuming all educators unfairly stigmatized students at risk was inaccurate. The point of sharing this with the class was to ensure they understood clearly the consequences of their actions in the classroom. This included understanding that both teacher and program responses to their actions were not personal attacks but reactions to the students' actions. Thus, I defused the students' belief that they were being personally attacked when disciplinary issues arose. Through the clarity we established, students began to take responsibility for their actions instead of becoming defensive or resistant, or interpreting people's responses as personal attacks. We also established a clear understanding of the role their actions had in their success.

By establishing clarity in the classroom, I effectively established a better line of communication with my students, avoiding many misunderstandings and unnecessary problems. The students learned to expect that I would give them my best effort in teaching to help them pass the GED, and that I would be fair with them. Clarity also prevented the students from "reading between lines"; there were no "gray areas" they could manipulate, even though some of these students were experts in finding loopholes. As a result of clarity, there was little room for misinterpreting anything we discussed in class. Ultimately, clarity was an effective tool in bringing the students and me closer together in a manner that further strengthened our success. Through clarity, the students respected and accepted the expectations we had established.

## REDUNDANCY

As stated in Chapter 2, redundancy includes repetition, reiteration, and reinforcement. I practiced redundancy in the classroom through multiple approaches to teach my students the core academic concepts and to support the learning style of each student. As Mojica (2006), noted, reiteration occurs "where the interpretation of some element in the discourse is dependent of another . . . whether they have the same referent or whether a referential relationship exists between them."[2] Therefore, I maintained

---

[2]Leonisa Mojica, "Reiterations in ESL Learners' Academic Papers: Do They Contribute to Lexical Cohesiveness," *The Asia-Pacific Education Research* 15, no. 1 (2006): 110.

the interconnectedness between each lesson and the core academic concepts. As one student noted, "We be watching video clips on YouTube, cool documentaries, we be reading song lyrics from 2Pac and this man be tying everything to the GED stuff." Thus, the concepts from the GED were taught numerous times but in different formats, allowing the students to understand the concepts in a variety of ways.

I presented every concept in a multitude of ways and, when possible, also tried to combine concepts in lessons (e.g., making inferences, identifying style and tone, and drawing conclusions). But whether I was teaching one concept or many, the lesson was usually short, concise, and engaging, designed to draw my students in to the learning process.

One concept that required redundancy for students to learn was making inferences. The Steck-Vaughn book gave two statements on making inferences. The first stated, "Sometimes when you read nonfiction, facts are only implied or suggested. In such cases you must figure out what the author is saying by using both stated and suggested information. This skill is called making inferences."[3] The second was, "Making an inference [means] using stated and suggested information to figure out an unstated idea."[4] Although these are good, the statements did not resonate with my students. These statements reflect the vernacular of the mainstream middle class. As such, they exclude entire groups of people who might easily comprehend the concept if it were explained in a different vernacular. My students needed an explanation that resonated with them, something more relevant to them that still maintained the academic meaning of making inferences.

In my first alternative lesson,[5] I asked students how they could tell someone they cared about was mad at them without being explicitly told. This immediately connected the lesson with their personal lives. Students' responses to my question varied:

- "Yeah, I can tell because they act differently."
- "Because the way they talk to me changes, so I know something is wrong."
- "It's hard to explain, but I can figure it out by the little things that change in them."

After they shared their views, I explained that although they had no solid evidence, they put the information they did have together to come up with their determination, and that in doing so, they were making inferences. Most of my students grasped the concept after this short exercise. Then we moved on to other examples of the same concept.

---

[3]Ellen Northcutt et al., *Steck-Vaughn GED Language Arts, Reading* (Austin, TX: Steck-Vaughn, 2002), 60.

[4]Ibid.

[5]See Chapter 6 for definition of alternative lesson.

I also used YouTube, DVDs, and video streaming to help my students understand concepts because movie scenes can be powerful tools to reinforce concepts. Before showing a scene, I always asked the class who had seen the particular movie I hoped to use. If the majority of the class had not, I felt the clip was new enough and fresh enough to stimulate learning. However, I always had scenes from other movies ready to use in case too many students in class had already watched my first choice. I did not provide my students with any background material or the story line. Instead, I asked students to be attentive as they watched the clip and to write down what they felt the people in the scene were feeling or thinking, and what they thought the movie could potentially be about. I typically selected emotional scenes that helped my students feel what was happening to the characters in the particular clip.

One clip I used in class to teach making inferences was from *Braveheart*, starring Mel Gibson. I showed 10 minutes from a scene in which William Wallace, accused of treason, is tortured. Wallace is asked to "fall to your knees now. Declare yourself the king's loyal subject and beg his mercy and you shall have it."[6] The consequence Wallace must face for not begging for mercy is being tortured before he is executed. In the scene, some people connected to Wallace are in the audience that has gathered to watch him die. The clip contains little dialogue.

After showing the scene, I asked the class a series of questions to help them extract inferences from the clip:

- "What do you think William Wallace was thinking or feeling besides the obvious physical pain?"
- "What were his two friends in the crowd thinking or feeling based on what you saw?"

I used similar questions, which might vary from class to class, to induce class discussions to reinforce their skills in making inferences to show students how they decipher things without fully knowing the facts or all of the information. When appropriate, I also used the clip to reinforce other concepts. In the case of this particular clip, I could incorporate the concepts of identifying style and tone, drawing conclusions, identifying plot, and analyzing character.

I then assigned homework that reiterated the concepts. In this case, the assignment was to write down a few verses from a song that the students felt had powerful meaning. They were not to include the name of the song in their lyrics. That way, students had to make inferences based only on the information provided. I collected the lyrics the next day, mixed them up, and redistributed them, making sure each student received a new set of lyrics. After the students read their lyrics, I randomly selected students to

---

[6]"Scene 20," *Braveheart*, directed by Mel Gibson (Los Angeles, CA: Paramount Studios, 1995), DVD.

share the lyrics and to explain what they could infer from what they had been provided. The students typically had fun with this assignment and were comfortable sharing their thoughts. In addition, they were simultaneously learning and practicing the concept of making inferences.

As the final step, students completed the few exercises and mini tests provided in the Steck-Vaughn book to make sure they grasped the meaning of the concept. I also integrated other mini tests from GED prep resources to make sure my students applied the concept consistently in a variety of materials.

Although such lessons seem tedious when written out, teachers can execute them quite effectively within the time constraints of most class periods. This is possible because the overall pedagogy helps teachers eliminate distractions and disciplinary referrals within class.

## ENTHUSIASM

The most difficult and exhausting aspect of the structure for me personally was enthusiasm. Although I was genuinely happy to be in the classroom with my students, sometimes it was difficult to conjure true outward enthusiasm. Still, I attempted to arrive to every class with an enthusiastic attitude.

On a typical day in my class, I greeted students at the door or acknowledged them as they walked into class and found seats. I did not pretend to be happy or excited but focused my enthusiasm with students on the everyday preparation for class and on getting them closer to passing the GED. I focused their goal of passing the GED into a form of "beating their adversary" to overcome an obstacle within their lives. The basis for my enthusiasm was the personal gains I knew they could achieve when they used education as an avenue for success. My students accepted this as a legitimate reason to be enthused about coming to class and about looking forward to taking their exams. This enthusiasm also allowed students to view me as their ally in their quest to overcome a standardized test that, like so many other exams in their lives, had proven to be an obstacle for them.

When presenting material to the students, I tried to make the lessons interesting by mixing them in with other concepts. I showed students my excitement in the ways I spoke about the material and connected it to them and their passing the GED. I was eager to answer student questions; when they asked questions, I exemplified that excitement to help minimize their fears. This fostered a fun learning environment for students while they were engaged with the core concepts needed to pass the GED exams.

On a more individual level, I showed my enthusiasm to my students through my authentic interest in what they had to say and what they were willing to share. I listened intently in our conversations, giving them feedback when appropriate. The HEP students, like so many students at risk, were not accustomed to having a voice in society; they were used to having their voice ignored because others were unwilling to listen to what they had to say. As enthusiastic as I was to listen to them, they were even more excited to share. They enjoyed sharing what they had to say with a person who was willing to listen and was not judging them in the process. Understand that my students were not my friends; the line between student and teacher was never blurred. I simply treated my students as human beings. I was excited to learn more about them, which helped me better prepare them to overcome the obstacle that stood before us.

However, some days I had difficulty being enthusiastic because I did not feel well physically, emotionally, or mentally. On those days, because I was authentic with my students, they noticed my lack of enthusiasm and inquired whether I was okay. This was a positive and exciting experience for me because these students typically did not spend time or energy worrying about how their teachers felt. Because I wanted to be genuine with them, I did not force my enthusiasm in the classroom. Doing so would have had negative consequences. My students were experts in seeing through superficial behavior. For them, reading people was a survival mechanism. They respected teachers who showed that they were not emotionless robots in the classroom but rather people who had good days and bad days just like them. Thus, establishing genuine enthusiasm with my students was more important and effective than being inauthentic. Over time, the norm in my classes was that, as a group, we were enthusiastic in working with one another five days a week until the day they took their exams.

## APPROPRIATE PACE

Determining appropriate pace is a task that requires constant attention throughout every semester. The first week of class, I focused on three main activities to determine appropriate pace: (1) asking the students about the pace of the class, (2) having students write about the class pace, and (3) giving students weekly exams or assessments to monitor the pace of student learning. Every day, I spoke individually with at least two students for a few minutes before and after class about the pace of the class. Speaking to students is extremely valuable. As their comfort level with me grew, they openly discussed their difficulties with the material we'd covered and what they had comprehended. Through these conversations, students unknowingly afforded me tremendous insight into what style of learning was most effective for them and how they comprehended the material. With this information, I altered my teaching to impact more students and to establish a consistent pace for the entire class. These discussions also served as unexpected sources of information about other students and more opportunities to achieve an appropriate pace for class.

Some students were not as willing as others to share their frustrations or lack of understanding because they were embarrassed or did not want to show me any sign of weakness. However, other students spoke on behalf of their peers as they told me how they were helping other students during personal time. Through these conversations, I gained the information I needed to address the difficulties these quieter students faced in the curriculum. I also learned which students were more advanced in the curriculum from those offering help to those struggling. I often had the more advanced students answer questions from their points of view, thus offering different viewpoints of the concepts being taught in class. This not only helped the rest of the students but also solidified the understanding of the advanced students.

I used a weekly writing assignment, a one-page reflection on class progress, to determine if the pace was too fast or too slow. This gave my students an avenue to vent their frustrations regarding concepts, my teaching, supplemental material used, or any other obstacle that inhibited them from comprehending what was being taught. Before and after every written reflection, I reminded the class that my ability to teach them would only improve with their honesty, that my manner of teaching was not perfect, and that only with their help could I effectively prepare them to pass the GED. Sharing this was an important component in empowering them to become part of the teaching process and in validating their views in the classroom. As students became accustomed to writing, their comfort level increased. In turn, they became more candid in their reflections, which allowed me to solidify the most suitable pace for the class. By the third week of the semester, student responses about the class pace were fairly consistent.

My assessments were also designed to guide instruction. Through them, I could identify each student's strengths and weaknesses, rate of learning, and ways in which each student could best demonstrate that learning.[7] In addition, all students were required to participate in weekly official GED practice testing sessions. The mini tests and quizzes taken in class were directly created from GED practice questions and were timed to help students become comfortable with the time constraints of the official GED. These assessments and methods, combined with daily discussions with students during and after class, helped me to determine the appropriate pace of the class. Eventually, the class moved at a swift yet comfortable pace, allowing us not to feel pressured by time constraints.

## MAXIMIZED ENGAGEMENT

Although the administrators strongly emphasized engaging our students in class, the idea of maximizing engagement was easier than its implementation in my classes. I did much self-reflecting concerning how I engaged

---

[7]See Samuel J. Meisels et al., *Thinking Like a Teacher: Using Observational Assessment to Improve Teaching and Learning* (Boston: Allyn and Bacon, 2002).

the class and how I could improve this engagement throughout the semester. I found that connecting concepts through both my students' life stories and my own was key in engaging my students. For example, when discussing symbolism, I provided examples of symbols from my life. I shared that to me a negative symbol was police officers or any type of law enforcement because as a young man, I had negative experiences with them. When I was growing up, law enforcement symbolized corruption; they were bad people, not the good guys they represented for most other members of society.[8] I then asked my students to share symbols from their lives. The students were eager to share their stories and, without realizing it, became intensely engaged in the class. This process fostered the development of positive rapport with the students as well.

Maximized engagement turns the classroom into a place in which students feel free: free of judgment and harsh punishments because of their perspectives and experiences, and free to engage in their own learning processes. Class was focused solely on neither the students' views of the world nor their development toward passing the GED exams. Rather, maximized engagement included stimulating students to share parts of themselves and to learn about others and about me in class. Thus, engaging students became a surprisingly trouble-free, enjoyable task.

Two activities that were particularly successful in maximizing engagement were Monday discussions and student presentations. Every Monday during each semester, my first class began with a discussion about each student's weekend activities. Because I inquired about their weekends, the students began inquiring about mine as well. Students were also assigned presentations about their favorite songs (limited to two songs per student). Students were typically very excited to share what they titled "a piece of myself" with the class. After playing their songs to the class, the students explained the meanings of their songs and their importance to them. I paid close attention during these presentations, provided positive feedback, and tried to help the students express themselves when they struggled.

I also asked questions about the presentations based on core connections to the curriculum. The class covered concepts such as interpreting theme, interpreting figurative language, making inferences, finding the main idea, restating information, identifying style and tone, and recognizing author's point of view. Students had to express their opinions, feelings, and points of view, which were also restated within the lessons. As with all of the assignments, the presentations led to a writing exercise that allowed students to implement aspects of their last four textbook units (sentence structure, organization, usage, and mechanics). The presentations also strengthened the overall rapport between the students and me, as one student noted: "I don't feel judged. You listen to me and you respect me. This is all I have ever asked from people and teachers."

---

[8]See Appendices A and I for additional examples.

Maximized engagement was not simply a matter of students doing work in my class or contributing to class discussions. It was about students feeling that our time together was not simply a class or the teacher's class but our class. They took ownership and had a sense of belonging that was established by asking for their input about how continually to improve the class (e.g., make things more interesting, improve lessons, incorporate new material). Many students made suggestions to improve the class; I not only listened but also, in many instances, implemented their suggestions. Although students typically noticed when their ideas and comments were used in class, I also acknowledged and thanked them for the suggestions during class. Acknowledgement kept students engaged in the class because they became part of the evolution of our class. Through their ideas for improvement, students also became more invested in their own learning process. Thus, student input is an intricate part of class; their insight needs to be respected, whether or not we agree with them.

Our position in class is not to demean or belittle their ideas. We are there to help students develop critically by expanding on their ideas to afford them educated and more encompassing perspectives. As they share their views, contribute to lessons, answer questions, and help others, they will develop a sense of belonging in class. Many students will feel valued because they will sense that you authentically value them. Your class should be a place where students belong rather than just a place where they take up space and waste time. For many students at risk, having a place where they feel they belong and where they are not viewed or treated as burdens contributes to their willingness to learn and keeps them engaged in the classroom.

Through maximizing engagement, students become an intricate part of the learning process rather than simply audience members who absorb everything a teacher presents. Students will spend their time and energy being engaged in what is discussed and shared, all of which will ultimately connect back to what is being taught in the classroom. Students will dedicate very little energy to disrupting the learning process, and they won't be distracted. Because they will remain engaged, students will not count the seconds they are in class; the time spent in class will simply breeze by—a major victory considering that students at risk would normally complain about the length of the class and about their boredom or lack of interest. Thus, maximizing engagement is critical to the ultimate success of our students.

# 5

## *Flexibility, Adaptability, and Effort*

**R**elating to students and teaching students a set curriculum using personal connections are two completely different things. I had to seize on my students' eagerness to learn by integrating the curriculum they needed to pass the GED. As I applied the concepts of my pedagogy, I truly grasped the necessity of S.C.R.E.A.M. combined with flexibility, or S.C.R.E.A.M.+F. I also realized that flexibility and Meyer's characteristics of a successful teacher, which I define as adaptability, were similar. In this chapter, I discuss the characteristics of flexibility, adaptability, and effort and their importance to student success.

Before beginning my first semester at HEP, the recruiter told me that I needed to "do something different" from the kinds of things the students had done in their previous schools if I was going to help them succeed. The assistant director cautioned me that "entirely traditional approaches towards these students will not be effective." I struggled to get my students to learn the material. Even though they were engaged and well behaved in the classroom and I had established a positive rapport with them, they were not learning as much as they needed to learn in the short time they had to prepare for the GED.

I became frustrated and, in a few instances, even lashed out at the class. On one occasion, when that happened, my students asked me what was wrong and why I was acting differently. I shared my frustration with them regarding their scores and blamed myself because I knew they were working hard. The students were pleasantly shocked when they heard me give them recognition for their hard work, but they felt I was being too hard on myself. In class that day, we brainstormed what I could do to help them improve their grades. We finished the day with no clear solution but had latched on to the idea of being flexible in the classroom.

## FLEXIBILITY

That night, I altered my lesson plans to create a clearer way for students to understand and learn the concepts in the class. I decided to teach some lessons through games, allowing students to work and compete in groups. I also had students participate at the chalkboard to teach and share their ideas and understanding of the concepts and skills they were learning. We went from a predominantly lecture- and individual-based learning environment to one that encompassed working in groups of various sizes, students teaching concepts (with assistance when needed), and participating in more interactive activities such as games to reinforce learning. To a visitor, the class might have seemed chaotic, but it was an active, student-engaged, student-centered learning environment. After only two weeks, I noticed that students were scoring better on assessments and that class averages were rising considerably. This trend of rising scores continued throughout the semester as I continued to change and modify lessons.

An example of a modified lesson is allowing a student to join instruction based on his or her own experiences. For instance, one of my quieter but engaged students asked me if he could explain to everyone what sentence structure meant and why it was needed. I gladly handed him the floor and sat with the rest of the class, paying close attention to his lesson. The student introduced the idea of "structure in the hood." Everyone knew and understood the rules or structure of their neighborhoods without having to think twice. He expanded the idea, saying that in their own neighborhoods, they knew where it was safe, where the violence happened, where the drugs were, where the police hid, and where the different people hung out. When their neighborhood structure was "off," they could tell or identify it without having to ask anyone. He reminded the class that although outsiders thought their neighborhoods were crazy, the students could make sense of them because they knew the structure. If they did not know the structure of their hoods, they might be not only lost but also in danger at times.

The student transitioned from neighborhood structure to sentence structure, explaining that sentences make sense when students write them or read them and recognize errors in them. He then wrote four sentences on the chalkboard and asked the class to determine if something was wrong with each sentence and, if so, to point out what was wrong. To others, the hood example might have been confusing or meaningless, but to his peers, the lesson made perfect sense. The students were intrigued and receptive, and they participated. Toward the end of his lesson, I joined him to expand further on sentence structure. Thus, through flexibility, this young man became empowered, leading and teaching the entire class.

Although teachers might think such changes will take an abundance of effort or time, a few days making alterations can make a difference. Besides the improvement in test scores, students also provided ideas for modifications, which reduced my preparation time and the time spent on discipline within the classroom.

Flexibility is also crucial when something that works with one group of students does not work with another. I had established Real Talk sessions focused on experiences of racism and class discrimination. The majority of the students had revealed fairly consistent terministic screens, and I had developed an effective structure with which I was comfortable. However, when I tried to apply these lessons with a new class, I did not receive a positive response. The new set of students divulged perspectives that revealed discriminatory views of other racial and social class groups rather than personal experiences. Thus, my previous structural focus was irrelevant and ineffective. I restructured many of my lessons, Real Talk discussions, and reviews to emphasize the creation and implementation of stereotypes and the negative impact they have on people. The students were much more receptive to the new lessons and became more involved with them, making it easier for me to teach this particular group of students.

Flexibility also means keeping the internal structure of the class varied. Within a one-hour class, keep students engaged by changing the lessons, games, lectures, and type of work performed in class. Although I followed a general structure, the daily activities in my classes were different to ensure students were not bored or "shut off" to what I was teaching them.

Because students will not always be receptive to every lesson as planned, try not to approach a class one dimensionally. For example, when you are delivering any lesson in the classroom, you must pay close attention to your students' receptiveness and needs. If students are not interested in what you are teaching them, be willing to change the examples or lessons you are using. Ask students if they are interested in what you are teaching them and, if not, why they are not interested and how you could make it better for them. Often we as educators feel an obligation to have to be "right" or know all the answers, but we can't and don't know everything. In fact, there will be times that students are better versed in something than the teachers. By openly inviting students to contribute, you are allowing yourself to be flexible and amenable to shifting what you are teaching in "real time," putting your students' needs in the forefront of your teaching.

Incorporate things in your classroom that push you beyond your comfort zone. We all have specific styles in which we deliver our lessons, and we typically stay within that style. But at times, our students need us to push ourselves for the sake of their learning. For example, if you are a serious teacher who seldom laughs, perhaps you would be willing to try a day where you are lighthearted and funny in class. Or, if you are a teacher who is always making students laugh, perhaps you take a day where you focus on things in a more serious manner. The point is to remain flexible on all fronts and push yourself to be multi-dimensional.

In the early stages of incorporating flexibility, I was nervous with the changes I made because I felt that I was going against the norm of what other teachers do with students. However, I quickly realized that it was not about doing what other teachers were doing but about doing what was effective for my students. I felt the most pressure when I realized that students were losing interest in my lesson and that their focus on what I was teaching diminished. Almost instinctively, because I did not want to admit defeat or ineffectiveness, I found myself imposing ineffective and boring lessons on my students. It is difficult for teachers to accept that we are not effective at times in the classroom; it is simply easier for us to blame the students. I learned that to try something different, I had to be flexible and honest with my students. The sheer honesty and willingness to find something else was more effective and paid tremendous dividends not only in students' test scores but also in our relationship in the classroom.

## ADAPTABILITY

Adaptability requires attention to your students' needs and to their levels of understanding. It is important to incorporate appropriate assessments throughout the semester. Just listening to the students during our class lessons is one way to assess their learning. For example, during an alternative lesson on making inferences, comparing, and contrasting, my students struggled to grasp the concepts. I led our discussion toward students' dream cars and had the students do an in-class side-by-side evaluation of three of these cars. I had already extracted the three most popular dream cars from previous Real Talk discussions we had had in class. Students used the Internet to gather information about prices, engines, and performance; descriptions of the interiors and exteriors; lists of safety features; and reviews by both experts and car owners. They also found photos of each car. They presented the information via the overhead projector and then proceeded to evaluate the three cars.

This type of alternative lesson engaged the students; subtly reinforced the concepts of inference, comparison, and contrast introduced in the initial lesson; and helped eliminate their confusion about those concepts. This lesson did not require hours of preplanning. The students had already given me the information about their dream cars through our Real Talk discussions. The Internet resources were instantly available. This impromptu lesson took little more than listening to student responses to recognize their confusion and the ineffectiveness of my planned lesson and a willingness to be flexible and change the lesson context while still delivering the necessary lesson content.

Adaptability is also key in meeting the needs of different classes. Don't force students to adapt to rigid lesson plans. Instead, if needed, adapt lessons and ideas from one semester to the next and from one group of students to the next. I found that allowing students to have a voice in the class helped me identify what was successful with them and what was not. Then I tweaked the lessons to ensure student success. This ultimately allowed me to teach the students the material and be within Meyer's successful teacher characteristic of being able to teach the students. Although flexibility and adaptability are a focus of my pedagogy, I also try to instill in my students that these are characteristics they need to work with different types of instructors, employers, and co-workers.

Students are extremely diverse in their personalities, styles, and interests. We as teachers must adapt to the different personalities and groups of people that our students represent. Although I saw many teachers attempt to force, intimidate, punish, or ignore students who were not the type of person with whom they felt they could relate, it is far better to adapt to your students. I tried not to superimpose my views or interests on my students or make assumptions about them. Instead, I listened actively to gain insight into who they were as people. I adapted to students who at first glance seemed annoying and irritating, or who were standoffish or aggressive toward me. I attempted to build positive relationships through my pedagogy with students and learn about their personalities. I was able to connect with them and build positive relationships wherein they trusted me and I trusted them by using Real Talk. Thus, I connected with a multitude of students—including the young, openly gay man in my class who felt he couldn't trust heterosexual men, and the angry woman who hated men because of tragic negative experiences throughout her life—rather than only a select group that were most similar to me as a person.

At times, perhaps unconsciously, we tend to connect with students with whom we can talk easily, and to alienate those who challenge us when we speak with them. We may not be able to connect with students at risk as easily as we do with others. There are a multitude of reasons why this is so. Students at risk might distrust authority figures because of their negative personal experiences with them or because of substance abuse. They might be reclusive due to bullying or other negative experiences, have become cynical toward teachers and the education system, be apathetic due to their life experiences, feel bored with and disengaged from school, among other reasons. But it is for these same reasons that it is absolutely crucial that we tirelessly attempt to authentically connect and engage these students, serve as a source of empowerment for them, offer them a safe place within our classroom, and potentially find solutions to their struggles for them to become successful not only in school but also in their lives. It is the students that need us the most that will push us away the most. Don't let this be a deterrent; instead, let it be a signal for us to make sure we are committed to adapt in the necessary ways to make sure we are successful with all of our students.

## EFFORT

Effort in teaching students refers not to completing the bare minimum with students, but to being truly available at times that are convenient for the students. Spending extra time with students can be a better use of time than preplanning or disciplining. Make time to work with students who have questions about classwork or to discuss personal issues affecting their performance in class. Meet with students before class, during class, and after class. The extra time spent with students is extremely useful in creating connections, making your job easier and the classroom more enjoyable for all.

Taking some extra time with students is often minimal compared with the powerful results that it yields. Often questions about the class that the students thought were difficult or overwhelming were simple for me to answer, given my knowledge of the curriculum and my professional preparation. Thus, I could quickly and effectively work one-on-one with my students. Their confidence increased, while their doubts decreased. One student commented, "[Paul] has always made time for me, and I really appreciate that. It makes me work harder in his class." If you are unable to meet with students, use clear and honest communication to avoid offending them. For example, instead of telling students that I was busy, I explained the specific reason I could not meet with them. This was simple and subtle but greatly appreciated by my students, who shared how different it was to meet a teacher who made time for them. Thus, over the course of our 12 weeks together, these small investments of time paid tremendous dividends in positive relationships.

In the Pedagogy of Real Talk, effort and involvement are crucial to student success. In many cases, students viewed the time I spent with them as a sign of respect and caring. These feelings, in turn, inspired many of my students to put forth more effort in their studies and preparation to pass the GED. When they saw they were continually improving in their assignments, exams, understanding of material, and overall critical development, it felt like a personal victory.

Many people think that teachers have a positive attitude toward all of their students, but I have found that this is not always true. We assume that people become teachers because they like students. However, as one teacher posed, how do we maintain a genuine positive attitude with a group of challenging students at risk who seemingly do not want to learn and have no regard for their teachers? It can be extraordinarily difficult to maintain a positive attitude toward some students at risk, given their involvement in self-destructive behavior inside and outside of the classroom. It is important to acknowledge their challenging behavior and discuss its consequences rather than ignore their problems. Ignoring issues only exacerbates them. I was determined to maintain a positive attitude and to make every student aware that I believed in their ability to turn their lives in a more positive direction. Know about existing resources (e.g., counseling, substance abuse programs, gang prevention programs, women's shelters) to help them deal with the issues they face, but don't impose these things on your students. Awareness and positive feedback help students see their lives as hopeful.

It's critical to maintain a genuine positive attitude toward the work that the students do in class. My students often became frustrated with their work because, historically, many of them were not successful students. It frustrated them that they did not grow by leaps and bounds in the classroom. They blamed themselves, referred to themselves as stupid, became frustrated and lashed out at others, accused the lessons they were learning of being worthless, and even blamed me for not helping them enough. Although I could easily have become cynical and disregarded them, I understood that my students were no different from other people who, when they grow frustrated or do not understand something, become difficult to be around. My frustration grew as theirs did, but rather than lash out, I simply smiled and told them things were going to be okay. I shared my frustration with them and assured them that we would find a way for them to succeed. I just needed them to remain receptive and not to give up. Success results from finding the best avenue for students to allow them to understand and succeed in class.

# 6

---

# *Terministic Screens and Real Talk Discussions*

Teaching students at risk is typically very challenging. As the pedagogy is slowly but surely implemented, however, students at risk will reveal themselves as some of the brightest, engaging, and most fulfilling people you will have the privilege to serve. Crucial to this revelation is understanding their terministic screens.

## TERMINISTIC SCREENS

Although dialogue is useful and beneficial in gaining glimpses of students' terministic screens, Real Talk is ultimately the key to the most encompassing and insightful understanding of their terministic screens and thereby of their insight and lives. This understanding is crucial to the overall, long-term success in working with students at risk in the classroom. As discussed earlier, you cannot use Real Talk on a daily basis to increase students' passing rates. When you do use it, keep notes, both mentally and physically, about what you learn from your students to more effectively incorporate their terministic screens.

I used terministic screens in two specific ways. The first was in the continual creation of new and relevant Real Talks throughout the semester. We will discuss Real Talks further later in this chapter. The second was in the creation and implementation of alternative lessons. An alternative lesson is one in which the content standard(s) from the curriculum is combined with the students' terministic screens or with societal issues outside the classroom that connect with students' terministic screens. When we lack students' terministic screens or when we wish to diversify things in the classroom, we must introduce societal issues with which students can connect, issues that students find interesting or that will generate their interest.

Alternative lessons resonate with students, inducing their involvement in the lessons, much more than listening to a teacher deliver a lesson by talking at the class. Alternative lessons connect students to material that typically seems irrelevant, leading them to become more receptive to the material and making the material less threatening or boring. Although these lessons often begin with material seemingly far removed from the curriculum content, the connection to the material the students must learn eventually becomes quite clear. Students typically flesh out their personal connections with the alternative lesson as they understand more clearly how the material connects to their lives at some level.

In my classes, some students shared negative perspectives about specific racial groups based on past experiences or incidents. I used their terministic screens on race relations as a foundation for an alternative lesson. We began with a 10- to 15-minute discussion on their negative experiences with other racial groups. I also shared experiences I had had with other racial groups. Within our discussion, many students shared disturbing experiences and the strong emotions they still felt about them. I extracted a few of the generalizations some of them had made about entire racial groups based on one or two experiences they had had with a specific individual. The students gave examples of situations in which they felt they had been discriminated against. One of these incidents was based on the students' comparison of how an individual had approached them in a department store with how the same individual had approached others in the same location. When the situations were ambiguous, they deduced that they were victims of racial discrimination.

As I highlighted these statements, I transitioned into the curriculum, connecting it to their experiences. I created an alternative lesson using the core concepts of comparing and contrasting, identifying style and tone, making inferences, understanding motivation, and drawing conclusions. We discussed how these concepts were all used within their experiences with racism.[1] They compared and contrasted their treatment in the department store with the treatment of the other people. They compared and contrasted the style and tone the person who approached them used in speaking to them. In the ambiguous situations, the students inferred and drew conclusions regarding racial discrimination against them. I then

---

[1]The title of this lesson was "Have You Ever Been a Victim of Racism? How Do You Know You Have Experienced Racial Discrimination?"

explained that although I could see what had motivated their dislike for specific groups, they were using an incorrect generalization in assuming that the actions of a few people from a specific group reflect the actions of every person in that group. We then used the GED Steck-Vaughn book and other resources to review different passages to identify the same concepts. In the final component of the lesson, students read short stories regarding people who had been victims of racial discrimination within the United States and the impact it had had on their lives. Thus, as a result of using students' terministic screens regarding race relations, the students were extremely engaged and willingly did the work to identity and use the concepts taught within the lesson.

One of the most challenging things teachers face in any writing class is getting students to write. Writing is a scary process for students for a multitude of reasons; some of them won't even write their names, let alone an entire sentence. The key for me was to get them to write before we tackled the rules of successful writing. Through Real Talks, I learned that many of my students had developed skills, talents, and tremendous inner strength because of their life experiences. However, they had been overwhelmed with unfair, cruel, and negative critiques from people in positions of power within their lives. Through their terministic screens, the world was a place where they had to hide what they were good at doing. Therefore, I created an alternative lesson that was a writing assignment, based on students' terministic screens, titled "The Me You Don't Know."

As part of the assignment, I asked them to read a one-page paper to understand what I was asking of them. The paper was about an anonymous man who had been belittled, mentally terrorized, and treated like a monster because he did not fit in where he grew up. The young man was extremely shy and lacked confidence. His physical appearance was quite different, even grotesque. However, no one knew his one major strength, not even those closest to him: He was a powerful public speaker who could captivate audiences. Speaking in front of audiences was the only place he felt free. When he was delivering an address, he did not worry about his personal deficiencies, about being considered physically grotesque or different from those around him.

After the students read the paper, I asked them what they thought the young man felt and whether they were surprised about his strength given how he felt about himself. Many students felt sorry for the guy because he was hurt. Some thought the story was sad because the man only felt free on stage. Others responded that they were very surprised that he could speak in front of audiences in a powerful manner even though he was personally insecure. As the class finished giving their thoughts, I announced, "The Me You Don't Know." At first, students were perplexed as I explained that I was the person in the story.[2] Then they smiled, laughed, and ultimately

---

[2]If teachers are not comfortable using themselves in this lesson, they may choose someone else.

understood that I was asking them to write about themselves. I was also specifically asking my students to share something that no one—or very few people—knew they could do well. To ensure their comfort level, I had them write anonymously. I also gave them no time restrictions to avoid unneeded pressure as they became more comfortable with writing.

I was pleasantly surprised when many of the students who typically were unwilling to write even one sentence wrote so much during one class period. Some wrote two and three pages to share their version of "The Me You Don't Know." Not only did I get them to write through this alternative lesson, but I also learned a great deal about them through their tremendous papers. My unassuming students were outstanding artists, musicians, athletes, charismatic leaders, and people with tremendous passion.

As we progressed, I used their papers to teach them how to transform them into the appropriate writing needed to pass the GED and to succeed overall academically. Their fear of writing dissipated over the course of the semester, and they began to see themselves as capable writers.

Thus, alternative lessons offer unlimited resources for teaching students the necessary material in their classes or standardized tests. They also offer opportunities to challenge their terministic screens. Through the particular lesson I used, I began confronting their terministic screen that teachers are not trustworthy, dismantling their hesitancy or fear in encountering people in authoritative positions.

## REAL TALK

Real Talk discussions are the most powerful tool in the pedagogy. Through them, you can speak with students on universal themes (e.g., sadness, anger, frustration, happiness, excitement) and tap into their terministic screens, passions, fields of expertise, and experiences to establish powerful connections. With my students, I used Real Talk in diverse ways, ranging from building connections with students to inspiring them, and from helping students focus or regain focus to linking students into curriculum standards they struggled with in class. Real Talk allows teachers to look beyond the superficial shell created in the traditional teacher–student relationship to see the person behind the student. In turn, students can see the person behind the teacher. Thus, we gain insight into each other, which leads to understanding our likes, dislikes, and, most important, our passions.

The expertise, interests, and passions of students will vary, ranging from musical talents such as singing, rapping, or playing an instrument to artistic expressions such as drawing or painting to active endeavors such as boxing, athletics, or customizing cars. One of the objectives in finding students' terministic screens, passions, interests, fields of expertise, strengths, and weaknesses is to pique their investment and involvement in class. As a result of Real Talk, students share the struggles and successes they experience in their everyday lives. This further enriches the classroom and helps educators to understand the reasons students struggle to succeed in school and to find ways to help them succeed despite their everyday struggles.

## Structuring Real Talk Discussions

Creating and delivering Real Talks can be exhausting at times because of their personal nature. But every discussion you facilitate will be worthwhile because it has a remarkable impact on the students and their learning. Real Talks give you the most insight into students' terministic screens, which you can use to create new and consistently more relevant Real Talks.

I designed the overall structure to integrate and implement Real Talk into classes in an unobtrusive, natural way. Real Talk should never be forced or approached in a manner that makes it seem artificial. Students see through such artificiality and lose their receptiveness and respect for us as teachers. Before the beginning of every semester, I reviewed the curricular standards. I then selected a diverse, broad set of universal themes to use in my classes. In determining these themes, I drew on my personal life experiences or those of friends, loved ones, or people I learned about to create and select my Real Talks. The next set of Real Talks I created was not necessarily directly connected to the curriculum. Instead, these talks were focused more on making overall connections and enhancing relationships with my students in the classroom.

As mentioned previously, I used the first Real Talk strategically on the first day of class to debunk the notion of the teacher as an entity in the classroom. I showed my students that I was a real person willing to reveal parts of myself to connect with them as people rather than as students.[3] This initial Real Talk established the nontraditional approach I would use to teach and my expectations of my students. I exemplified teaching not simply as a job but as my personal connection to education. I used it to show my desire to connect each student to education in a manner best suited to that person instead of forcing my students to learn in the manner imposed on them by so many teachers in their past. Starting the semester in this way typically garnered a powerful, positive response: gaining the respect of my students. Earning their respect was a positive step in building a relationship through which I could effectively teach and students could willingly and openly learn.

Other Real Talks were also implemented strategically throughout the semester. For example, mid-semester, students were typically tired, homesick, and frustrated with school. Keeping them focused on their schoolwork was challenging. However, it was also the perfect time to

---

[3]See Appendix B.

interject a Real Talk to help them overcome this mid-semester lull. However, as I looked for opportunities to use Real Talks appropriately, I understood that overuse could minimize their effectiveness. By placing Real Talks strategically, I kept students wanting more, anticipating the next "special" talk.

I connected some Real Talks directly to the curriculum by tying them into the material students needed to know. Doing so lessened the threatening impact of the curriculum and established student receptiveness to the material. These Real Talks were not alternative lessons. Although the two are somewhat similar, alternative lessons have a far more specific but equally important role within the pedagogy: to connect curriculum content directly with the class. Real Talks have a complementary role to alternative lessons, as does the rest of the pedagogy. Thus, when I tied Real Talks to the curriculum, I placed them strategically where students needed the most help or motivation, typically involving concepts or sections in the curriculum that students usually found difficult.[4] Through the talks, students found the material more approachable and enjoyable. Students were also more able to relate to the material because the talks were connected to their terministic screens.

As most teachers do, I created some of these Real Talks as part of my preparation for new classes. When creating Real Talks before meeting my students, I focused on universal themes (e.g., happiness, frustration, emptiness, triumph) and connected these themes to myself. My overall objective was to connect with students on a universal and personal level. Even though I did not personally know my students, I could count on them having experienced happiness, anger, frustration, eagerness, fear, hate, and love, regardless of what had caused them to feel these things. The personal component involved sharing various aspects of my personal life. Regardless of who my students were, the personal component was dependent on my own truth and personal testament because I could not depend heavily on my students. Both the universal and the personal components are the beginning parts of all Real Talks structurally and are important tools that I relied on as I first met my students and got to know them. I also had to remain flexible when implementing any of the Real Talks created prior to meeting my students, adjusting or changing things to ensure appropriateness and relevancy for my students.

Based on what I learned about my students from Real Talks, I created additional Real Talks to add to the set. This allowed me to replace Real Talks I'd used previously with new ones based on the insights I'd gained into my students. By creating reusable, adaptable Real Talks, I developed a deep pool from which to draw to match the needs of my students at any given point in the semester.

---

[4]See Appendix A.

The final component of structuring Real Talks is learning to trust yourself enough to use Real Talks at a moment's notice, otherwise known as the teachable moment. Rather than letting these moments simply pass by, capture them with Real Talks to enhance and connect with the students' learning experience. Although you may have experienced many teachable moments, you have to learn how to incorporate Real Talks systematically to maximize these opportunities.

When students shared things or certain topics arose that stimulated a Real Talk moment, I realized that I had to take ownership and accept that no one knew my class better than the students and I did. I became comfortable and flexible enough to put aside or modify any lesson or activity to incorporate the ad hoc Real Talk. I looked for opportunities to connect my life experiences to what students were saying to connect everything back to them. Although I did not do this every day, these Real Talks were wonderful supplements to keep us connected throughout the entire semester.

After every new spur-of-the-moment creation, I documented the Real Talk for potential future use. Doing so also contributed to the body of knowledge I was building concerning my Real Talk discussions with students. That information served in the creation of additional Real Talks for future classes based on sharing powerful components of actual students' lives with future students. Of course, I always ensured the anonymity of my students in these Real Talks. Names and dates were never included to maintain anonymity.

As with everything within the Pedagogy of Real Talk, Real Talk itself has to be flexible to accommodate diverse sets of students. You can incorporate Real Talks for a number of reasons, ranging from connecting with students overall to connecting specifically to concepts or curriculum standards to helping students overcome the obstacles they face throughout the semester. Real Talks allow you to be as encompassing as possible in teaching students. They afforded balance and helped me avoid becoming the overbearing, emotionally draining teacher in the classroom that students disregard.

Preparing Real Talks before meeting my students was crucial to establish the purpose of Real Talk in the classroom. Developing the ability to use Real Talks when there were teachable moments was a powerful component as well. Besides the strategically placed Real Talks (beginning, middle, and close to the end of the semester), the number of Real Talks I used with my classes was best determined from semester to semester as I got to know each set of new students. Although I established dates for using Real Talk, I always remained in tune with my students and receptive to their needs to determine how and when I used Real Talks.

Overall, Real Talks served an important role in class on multiple levels, although I never solely relied on them to teach my students. Implementing these discussions at a moment's notice also took time to master but ultimately strengthened my success as a teacher and my students' success in class. Through Real Talks, both preplanned and spontaneous, I effectively helped my students increase their passing rates.

## The Effects of Real Talks

Several students enlightened me about the impact of Real Talk in the classroom. Many students defined their former teachers as "fake" and stressed the importance of teachers who were "real" with them. One student articulated the clearest explanation of a fake teacher:

> First of all, they don't want me in the class and the way they treat me I can tell they don't like me. Teachers have tried to talk to me about shit other than school, but they feel sorry for me, judge me, and try to tell me what to do. They don't "feel me," care, or understand my struggles and pains. They were about how they sound and look to others not about really helping me out. It's about what they gain by trying to help me and I can see right through all that. They never really put themselves out there so I could see who they truly are. Shit, Paul, they focus on supposedly trying to help me, but they always keep their judgmental eyes on me to see how I respond. I am not stupid and neither are the other students, but this is what we have always dealt with, these fake ass teachers our whole lives.

This student's explanation characterized the opinions that many of my students openly and eagerly shared about teachers. Their perspectives of fake teachers led to their acknowledgement of real teachers. When any of the students in my case study discussed an effective instructor, they used that term: *real*. The realness factor stemmed from our in-class discussions of real-life feelings, emotions, and events.

However, my approach in treating and teaching students was not the only factor that made my class seem real. Students identified the specific, strategically placed lectures fostering open discussions as the thing that made the class seem real. One student described these lectures, which I later termed Real Talk:

> He [Paul] connects everything in class to real life stuff that we have all experienced somehow. His class inspires because of the kind of things we talk about. The subjects we talk about are just so inspirational to me and it makes me feel like I can do anything. He is so inspirational to me when he drops his Real Talk on the class.

Another student commented,

> He always talking about that real shit. He tells it like it is and lets us say what we want in the class as well. He does not hide anything from us when doing his Real Talk and it really opens me up to listening and sharing my real life situations outside of HEP. I wish teachers would have done what Paul does when he does Real Talk in class.

This student's comments highlight that my perspective or experience matching hers didn't necessarily matter. It was the willingness to "not hide" and to listen to what the students had to say.

Using Real Talk in the classroom helped me tremendously in keeping my students focused, dedicated, inspired, and driven. Such characteristics are rarely representative of students at risk. One student stated,

> He [Paul] really breaks things down so I understand them. He gives examples straight from his life and our lives (students) as well. Like not exact experiences from our lives but shit that we can relate to in life. Like he talks about the struggles in life, being broke, working hard and not getting nowhere, experiencing racism, and just all kinds of shit. Every time it's different. I mean, I can really connect with that stuff. It keeps me interested in what is going on in class because you never know when that real stuff is coming.

Real Talk created genuine interest in the class that helped maintain students' attention and focus on what they were supposed to learn. I integrated multiple Real Talks throughout the semester to keep students alert and constantly to include their thoughts, feelings, and emotions in our class culture. The students expressed looking forward to the Real Talk discussions, which made them an integral part of the class:

> He just is on some real shit. He really teaches us about life, how to get ready for the future and what's on the GED. It's strange because he combines everything so well in our classes. I love it when he gets in front of the class and he leads our special talks. He digs deep and gets us all sayin' some of the deepest shit I have ever heard in a class. I mean he is right about shit when he talks about us having to deal with shit in the past and in the future but he keeps us motivated and ready to pass his classes. Our talks are a part of what makes the class so real to me and why I love going to class.

With some Real Talk discussions, I tied the conversations back to the core concepts by reintroducing them within the discussion. For example, when one student led a Real Talk on pain, I connected it to the concepts of summarizing major ideas and analyzing tone. I did this by asking students to summarize how the student leader felt based on her tone of voice and the main ideas of her story. After students shared their thoughts, we transitioned to the lesson in the book that dealt with the concepts. One young man explained,

> Paul [is] always making class fun and interesting. Everything about class is like real life. It ain't no boring ass teacher shit, but some stuff that we can use when we go back home. I never been in a class that

I really understood until I came into this class. He be making it all easy for us and I be talking in that class because I want to learn more. I ask questions and tell everybody what I think because he don't hate on me. I feel like I am part of the class like I help by being involved and it helps me because I get my questions answered.

This particular student's enthusiasm in the class was only matched by his dedication to learning and passing the standardized test. Another student said,

He is just real. He don't judge me and works real hard for me and the class. He inspires me because I feel like I can do anything in his class and out in the world . . . It is just a lot of fun to be in his class. Learning things in his class is so easy because it is all about real life and we just be doing work in there like it is easy. Paul really cares about us and he pushes us to be the best so we can pass the GED. My confidence really has gone up because he keeps showing me that I really am smart and not dumb like teachers have always made me feel.

As the semester progressed, Real Talk stimulated students to share their thoughts and open up to the entire class. Students began taking initiative in class through leading the Real Talks. As they shared their experiences and connected them to the class, they inspired other students. I always tried to integrate these student-led discussions with the remainder of the class. I allowed and encouraged students to share their insights, which created a powerful, positive environment in the class. Thus, students took ownership of the Real Talk sessions.

Eventually, a physical impact of Real Talk in the classroom was apparent. When students thought or felt I was going to begin a Real Talk, they sat at the edge of their seats in anticipation of delving into our powerful talks. The students, like so many other students at risk, seldom remained quiet during class when a teacher was speaking, but Real Talk activated the "pin drop phenomenon": The students became so engaged and captivated that one could literally hear a pin drop in our classroom. For students who seldom dedicated their full attention to a teacher in the classroom to become so engaged gave tremendous insight into the effects of Real Talk with students.

Another interesting phenomenon accredited to Real Talk involved students who tested out of my classes. Only a handful of students occasionally qualified to test out of some of their classes. These students were typically more advanced academically compared with the majority of the students in the program. For example, some students who were very strong in reading might be struggling in the other four GED subjects (science, writing, math, and social studies). We allowed them to take the reading exam for the GED early so they could focus on their weaker subjects and have one less exam to stress about. The instructors and associate director determined which students qualified, based on their practice test scores, quizzes, and overall work. Students who tested out of a subject were no longer permitted to attend sessions for that class but were required to attend the classes of the subjects still needed.

What I encountered in my reading and writing classes with the students who tested out was both exceptional and humbling to experience as their teacher: Many of my students asked if they could continue to attend my class. They wanted to be a part of the lectures and learning we had created using this pedagogy. Most frequently, students identified Real Talk as the major reason they wanted to remain in my class. They shared that these special talks and the connections they felt in class were something they wanted to maintain—that those things helped them stay focused, motivated, inspired, and driven to do their overall work within the program. Having a student at risk who no longer needed or was permitted to attend a class but asked to continue to attend was almost unheard of not only within the program but also in any other academic setting.

Thus, what Real Talk was intended to do was clearly taking place and having an immense impact on the students. Although their test scores ultimately needed to reflect the impact of the pedagogy (as it clearly did in the study), it was equally important for me to have the perspective of the students. Students shared that our classroom was a safe haven, a place where they belonged instead of where they were treated like a burden in society. The students determined what was effective for them in the classroom, and their insight was of the utmost importance to me not only as a researcher but also especially as a teacher. The credentials I held that allowed me to stand before them and teach did not give me the insight to determine what they felt was best for them. Only with their help could I determine what suited them best in learning in my class.

Real Talk and alternative lessons are a breakthrough in establishing connections, generating interest in the subject matter, and providing an arena for students to learn material they normally resisted. As you learn more about your students, you must continue the sequence of adaptation and involvement of student experiences in the required content. You must continue creating powerful, relevant Real Talks and alternative lessons to captivate students and spark their interest in learning based on the information gleaned from Real Talks, students' terministic screens, and their personal experiences.

Thus, a group of students who were at one time considered apathetic, hostile, and cynical toward education will flourish and embrace the education process as they prepare to pass their classes and best prepare for standardized exams. No longer will they merely be going through the motions of attending class. They will be engaged and willingly share their understanding of the world. Thus, through their voices, the success of the Pedagogy of Real Talk is solidified.

# 7

---

# *Dealing With the Exceptions*

I t is likely that, even though you try your hardest, you will have difficulty reaching each and every student. I was not successful with every student in my classes. Even though I tried every strategy within my approach to connect with these students and help them, I failed to do so. These students, who constituted only a small number of the students I taught, were seemingly resistant toward me because of my specific pedagogical approach. Therefore, examining these cases has been essential to improving the approach.[1]

## THE CASE OF PB

PB, a quiet student who was always well dressed and groomed, had issues with being punctual for his first class of the day because, as he described, "I want to look good when people see me, and that takes time." He relied on his quietness to help him "fly below the radar." He did not disturb class, so when he did not attend class, he was easily overlooked. Although the program was very thorough and we held weekly meetings with the associate director to discuss student progress, we did not discuss PB until midway through the semester. He often did not

---

[1]Pseudonyms are used here to protect the identities of my students.

complete or turn in his work, did the bare minimum, and gave little effort in class to avoid attracting attention. He did not develop relationships with many of the other students and appeared more focused on the happenings in his hometown than in the program. Although he developed a few friendships within the program, he went to his home almost every weekend. PB was unique in terms of some of the issues he faced; regardless of what approach I attempted to connect with him, he remained resistant. I should have been more positive and flexible in my approach with him.

I pulled PB aside after class one day and told him I was concerned with what was going on with his work. He simply said that he was struggling and would try harder. However, I noted no improvement. I also noticed he was not receptive to the Real Talk discussions. He withdrew from the class by looking away or up at the ceiling as if in a daze. When students don't feel comfortable in school or in particular classrooms, they often withdraw, investing less in academic activities. I again spoke with him after class. He simply answered, "I don't know. I would just rather be back home when you guys start talking about things." Because PB was not receptive to any of our one-on-one talks regarding his work, he began to receive pressure through program consequences for his failure to comply with his HEP responsibilities. Still, he continued to do only the minimum.

As I reflected on PB, I realized I had not spent sufficient time with him during the semester to connect with him. The little time I did have was focused more on disciplinary issues. I had opportunities in class to foster a relationship with PB that I overlooked, either ignoring them or inadvertently creating negative situations rather than positive ones. For example, during Week 6 of class, I saw him smile and laugh for the first time. The students had been joking around with one another as usual. Trying to draw PB in, I implemented my inclusive approach by using one of PB's comments as an example. He had casually said, "I have all kinds of women on me here at MSU and I'm loving it." I thought it was a perfect opportunity to engage PB in a class lesson leading to a writing assignment and said to the class, "Well, it looks like we just found our topic to write about in class today." The class was quiet and seemed confused by my statement, so I referred to PB's comment:

> PB just said women are after him, and his tone of voice and body language seemed as if he was confident and comfortable with this. But, PB, you have spoken of your dedication to your girlfriend back home all semester. So, what is it, PB? Where is your dedication and passion? Your girlfriend back home or the girls here at MSU? So, class, that is your question. What is the focus of your passion and dedication?

Although the class understood the question, I had mistakenly helped the class at PB's expense.

I took great pride in providing clarity for students and creating questions from their personal lives. However, in this case, PB was offended by my using his personal life for a class assignment. When I looked over at him as I finished giving the assignment, I immediately saw that I had made a mistake. He looked down at the ground, turned red in the face, and hesitated to start the writing assignment. For the remainder of the class, he maintained stiff, uncomfortable body language.

He went to the associate director to discuss his feelings regarding my example. PB felt that I had singled him out in class. Although that had never been my intent, nonetheless, I had made PB feel that way. I had thought using his comment as an example would provoke him to start critically thinking about his own comments and engage in the class. I had been wrong. By offending him, I had shut him off to my class for the rest of the semester, and he continued to detach himself not only from my class but also from the entire program. At the end of the semester, he took the GED exams but did not pass several subjects, including the reading and writing tests. PB did not achieve his goal of earning his GED diploma.

## THE CASE OF JESSIE

My approach of openness regarding my life, often shared through the Real Talk discussions, worked against me with one particular student. Jessie was usually quiet and seemed shy and introverted. She was bright academically but lacked confidence in her abilities, which affected her performance in the classroom. Although Jessie was never a distraction in the classroom, I noticed that her performance overall declined over time. This was abnormal. When other students confided in me, I discovered that her shyness and lack of confidence were not the main issues in her academic performance. Jessie was scared of me. She found me intimidating. I had certainly not expected that and was determined to figure out how I had become a scary figure to her.

The students, more concerned with Jessie's performance than with keeping confidences, gave me several insights into what was happening. One of her friends said, "She thinks that you're scary because of all of the stuff you have been through in your life." The experiences that I sometimes shared with the class were terrifying and were different from those Jessie had experienced. Another student mentioned, "She thinks that you're too real to be a teacher, so it freaks her out." As the students continued to share their insights, I determined that through my Real Talk approach, I had intimidated Jessie.

Throughout the semester, I invited her to stay after class to discuss her performance. Each time, she asked one or two friends to stay with her, which I welcomed. Slowly but surely, Jessie revealed her feelings of intimidation. Once she said to me after class, "Your life sounds really scary.

I don't know how you don't just hate everyone." One day during a program luncheon, she said, "Paul, I did my work for you and I will turn it in today. I don't want you to be mad at me 'cause I'm nervous going to your class even when I do my work." I did not probe Jessie to elaborate further about how she felt. That would have been counterproductive for her.

As the semester progressed, I paid specific attention to Jessie during Real Talk discussions. Normally, students were receptive and engaged with Real Talk. However, Jessie typically seemed physically uncomfortable, her facial expressions revealing her discomfort. During one Real Talk discussion, I revealed that I had been an athlete as a young man, tying that information into the lesson for the day to establish a powerful connection with discipline and work while attending school. Jessie made a comment to her neighbor as I finished. When I asked her what she had said, she became extremely red in the face and said, "Nothing." I smiled and asked her to share with the class. "I said I would never want to make you mad because you would probably kill me," she replied. I smiled and told her that I would never be violent in an academic setting or with my students. She laughed nervously, and I could clearly see she was uncomfortable.

I was not successful in connecting with Jessie, nor was I able to speak with her in depth regarding her feelings about me and the effect I had on her preparation for the GED. Real Talk had not only been unsuccessful with Jessie but had also had a negative effect on her as a student. I continued using Real Talk because of the positive impact it had with so many students, but I could never find a solution for Jessie. She did not pass any of the five subject tests when she took the GED examination, and I acknowledged she had been negatively affected by my approach in reading and writing.

As I reflect on what I could have done differently with Jessie, specific examples come to mind. Instead of assuming that her quietness and lack of disruption meant that she was engaged, I could have taken the time to attempt to get to know Jessie in a more one-on-one manner. Perhaps I could have conducted small-group discussions with people around her with whom she felt comfortable. This would have given me the opportunity to connect with her and show her other parts of my life that were not as intimidating to her. I could have also attempted to create an assignment between Jessie and me where we communicated through email or writing letters to one another. This might have allowed her to more comfortably share what was on her mind and allowed me to share things about myself that would help counteract her feelings of discomfort and intimidation. I could have also paid closer attention to my Real Talks and her specific needs. As I share these ideas on paper, I think of our classic dilemma and colloquial phrase, "Hindsight is 20/20." But this should serve as an example and reminder of constantly being reflective as we teach our students because their success partially depends on our ability and willingness to constantly improve our teaching in the classroom.

# THE CASE OF LB

LB was the third student for whom my approach was unsuccessful. He was a young man who entered my class one week late, missing the orientation process. On entering my classes, he quickly established his resistance to my approach. When I delved into Real Talks or used creative lessons not directly from the curriculum, LB purposefully looked down or away from me. His body language and his purposeful avoidance of me as I spoke indicated his lack of interest. The lack of a positive student–teacher relationship between LB and me led to more disciplinary problems, which often occur when students do not feel a protective force and comfort stemming from student–teacher connections. As I reflected on LB, I believed my approach angered him and contributed to his resistance in the classroom.

As the semester progressed, signs of resistance became more clear and severe. During the class exercise comparing and contrasting students' dream cars, we connected the cost of vehicles to what students felt they needed to do to afford their dream cars. This discussion transitioned into the writing exercise regarding success in school leading to high-paying careers. As the writing assignment began, LB spoke out, "This is stupid because ain't nobody in here ever gonna own any of those cars." I smiled at him and said, "I never thought I would get out of the hood but I did." He responded, "Well, we all can't be like you and I rather just be me." I kept him after class and inquired about his negativity and disrespectfulness. He apologized and said he would watch himself and not let it happen again; that same week, however, he lashed out again.

The school had a strict policy about punctuality to class. If students are tardy to class, they are not permitted to enter the class. If tardiness becomes a recurring issue, then the students receive disciplinary consequences. One day LB walked in 15 minutes late, swinging the door open so hard it slammed against the wall, he grinned and said, "Hey, what's up? I'm here." I immediately stopped him from entering any farther into the class and asked him to go directly to the associate director's office to wait for me per procedure. When class ended, I met LB in private and told him that his attitude and behavior would not be accepted or tolerated in my classes. Then I asked him what I could do to help him adjust to prevent future incidents. He again apologized and simply stated that his behavior was his fault and would not happen again. I pointed out that apologies were not necessary, that we needed to prevent those behaviors from occurring again. He said nothing and sat hunched over, a serious look on his face as he stared at the ground. He simply said he was sorry and assured me there would be no issues after that day.

Other students made comments about his negative attitude that week and shared their frustration at being distracted because of LB's behavior.

He was being negative not only in class but outside class as well. As a result, many of LB's peers ostracized him. Very upset, one student told me,

> He talks a lot of shit about everyone in the program and thinks he is a bad ass. Paul, this guy ain't ready to change or be here and it makes me mad . . . This guy is digging a hole 'cause people are turning their backs on him because he is talking shit.

A female student told me,

> He talks about you all the time and how much he does not like you . . . that he is real and you are fake. He says that he ain't scared of you and that if you call him out on his behavior again, he going to call you out and put you in your place . . . He says that you don't really know anything about his life.

Unfortunately, as the students began to distance themselves from him, he lashed out even more.

I found it hard to help LB because his negativity and behavioral issues were not confined to the classroom. However, in the classroom, I continued to try to involve LB in assignments and discussions. I spoke to him either before or after class to connect with him. During Real Talks throughout the semester, he was resistant, as evidenced by his body language, facial expressions, and general lack of participation. Because he was disrupting the others from doing their work, I had to pull him aside repeatedly to discuss the issues. He apologized but never changed his behavior. I tried to remain flexible with him, but his behavior continued to spiral downward. He was also not receptive in any of his other classes and displayed inappropriate behaviors there as well. Ultimately, he was dismissed from the program because of his attitude, and I was not able to get him to accept responsibility for his actions.

## THE CHALLENGE TO TEACHERS

Although professionals frequently discuss the reasons students at risk fail, they seldom emphasize the ways we as teachers may fail our students at risk at times. Ogle (1997) suggested that teachers often fail to provide needed education to students at risk, offering them "a watered-down curriculum" when "they need to be engaged in interesting and challenging learning that goes beyond basic proficiencies" as all students should be.[2]

---

[2]Donna M. Ogle, *Critical Issue: Rethinking Learning for Students at Risk* (North Central Regional Education Laboratory, Centennial, CO, 1997), 1. Retrieved April 5, 2010, http://www.ncrel.org/sdrs/areas/issues/students/atrisk/at700.htm

Some of the most challenging aspects of being in the classroom with students at risk are not the challenges students present but the obstacles we as teachers create for our students and ourselves. I had grown accustomed to hearing some of my colleagues say that the difficulties students pose are not our fault as teachers. The fault lies with unmotivated, disconnected students. Like so many others, I easily fell into the trap of looking outward first when examining problems in my class rather than looking inward to see what I was doing wrong or what I could do to improve as a teacher. Even as a former student at risk who was constantly blamed for things in the classroom, I still fell into the trap as a professional, blaming students while knowing that I once sat in their seats and knew firsthand the negative impact of teachers who did not take responsibility for their actions in the classroom.

In analyzing how to be most successful with students at risk, we must begin with an analysis of ourselves as persons who teach in classrooms full of young people. Only after looking at ourselves in depth can we begin fully to understand the dynamics in our classrooms and to improve constantly to help our students succeed. As a graduate student, I heard scholars distinctly say, "You can't save them all, Mr. Hernandez, and if you think you can, you are being young and idealistic." When I grew weary and almost cynical due to the frustrations of teaching, the words of those scholars echoed loudly in my mind. I came to the realization that regardless of the outcome, I must give my students everything I have to make sure that, on my side, I do not cheat students by assuming or expecting that some will not succeed.

As teachers, we plant seeds in our students to help them grow into educated, successful, productive people within society. If we plant those seeds with the intention of watching them grow, then we have failed as teachers. Some students will blossom before our eyes, and we must remember the honor and privilege of seeing this happen. Other students will not begin their growth until well after our classes or even our lives. We must remember that as long as we earnestly give our entire effort, it doesn't matter if students prosper during our classes or 20 years after. Ideally, we want students to pass their classes and graduate, but there will be times when this is not the result. However, as long as students eventually benefit from any fraction of the teaching we offer, we have done our duty as educators.

Why does this occur? Sometimes, at the time they meet us, these students are simply not ready for change. I am a living example of such a student, never showing the significant impact a few teachers had on me because of the outstanding job they did in the classroom. It is partly because of these caring teachers that I achieved my doctorate.

Keeping this in mind, then, the challenge becomes using the Pedagogy of Real Talk to approach every student in class with the belief and aspiration that each and every one has the ability to engage, learn, and succeed.

If teachers don't have high expectations to challenge and engage their students to learn, these students will not succeed academically. Teachers provide the leadership and connections students need to succeed, but students only reach the expectations set forth for them. Given that teachers are the persons in classrooms that help lead students to learning and thinking critically, our responsibility as teachers is always to view ourselves critically as we learn to improve our craft of teaching.

Assumptions about our students will only hinder the learning process overall. For example, we cannot rely on assumed factors, such as race or background, to make connections. Students respond most dramatically to authenticity, both in their instructors' presentations of themselves and in their instructors' communicating their caring for their students. Thus, we must not only rigorously employ pedagogy but also constantly assess the appropriateness of its implementation. We can achieve this through constructive critical critiques of ourselves, constructive analyses of what we've created for the classroom, and the impact we have on our students. Then, perhaps years after we have initially taught these students in our classes, they will reference us as persons who changed their lives.

# 8

## *Implementing Real Talk in Any Classroom*

W e've discussed what the Pedagogy of Real Talk is and how it was implemented in classrooms. But is its successful implementation limited to the HEP program, or can this pedagogy be implemented in other classrooms? The answer is that the Pedagogy of Real Talk can be translated successfully into any classroom providing educators are willing to make the changes and connections necessary to engage their students in the process. In fact, since the creation of the Pedagogy of Real Talk, it has been adopted and used by hundreds of educators around the country, and results show that it can be used successfully by anyone who is willing to earnestly try and implement this pedagogical approach.

I have had the privilege of working with K–12, universities, community colleges, and educational nonprofit organizations around the world in training them in my approach. The pedagogy is not limited to any one type of institution; it can work within diverse settings where professionals want to enhance success with students. The applicability of the approach has ranged from administrators in universities seeking ways to teach their student-support staff how to connect with students at risk; centers for teaching and learning in community colleges trying to develop their faculties' teaching in the classroom; and nonprofit organizations that wanted to infuse engaging pedagogy in their programing. In diverse educational settings, the pedagogy has proven to be useful and effective.

In the following sections, I have provided more in-depth detail on how educators can be trained, the basic components of the pedagogy, establishing connections, Real Talk and alternative lessons, and the applicability of the training. The reason this approach was created is to ensure its usability by others so they could find success with their students. Additionally, this approach ensures that others can also maintain that success over time with as many students as possible. Therefore, the purpose of this chapter is to help educators understand how to apply the Pedagogy of Real Talk in their classrooms. I am hopeful that educators will incorporate the approach in its entirety or components of it to transform their teaching and become more successful in their chosen craft.

Educators must keep in mind that the only way we will continue to serve our students best is through continual professional growth. We must avoid the pitfall of becoming complacent with our teaching strategies. We must challenge ourselves to learn new things that we can feasibly apply in the classroom that will make an impact on our students, especially our students at risk. Through the Pedagogy of Real Talk, we can actively seek to connect with our students and learn from them. We can then combine what we learn with the material we must teach.

The examples in this chapter have been created after careful assessment of individual teachers to determine the structure needed to be successful in the classroom. I share this because school and teacher needs are the determining factors in creating a structure for training teachers in the Pedagogy of Real Talk. What is shared in this chapter should serve as a model to create such a structure more easily.

The fundamental aspects of the pedagogy were applied in all five subjects that compose the GED curriculum when I substituted for my HEP colleagues. Even though I used their teaching plans and materials, I could still apply the approach. Then, in the fall semester, the new teacher for the Spanish sections of reading and writing asked for help in implementing the pedagogy. As shown in Chapter 3, her students' passing rates increased dramatically compared with the students' passing rates during the two semesters taught by the previous instructor of those classes.

That fall I also met Ms. D, a high school teacher who had been teaching for 10 years. She was frustrated with her lack of success with students at risk and was willing to learn the Pedagogy of Real Talk. Ms. D was already a very good teacher when I first met her, yet she felt that there was room for growth in her approach to teaching. This set the tone for our work together. She was trained for an academic year, implementing the various strategies as she learned them. Each year, the district statistician analyzed student passing rates by teacher. Her student passing rate after her implementation of the pedagogy was 8.8% greater than her previous year's passing rate.[1]

Although I could easily apply my pedagogy in the classroom and explain it to others, I found that training someone else to use it consistently and effectively in the classroom was more challenging. One extremely

---

[1]See Paul Hernandez, "College 101. Introducing At-Risk Students to Higher Education," *NEA Higher Education Journal* Fall (2011): 2.

valuable lesson I learned from Ms. D was that my approach only worked with those willing to try it wholeheartedly, agreeing to push themselves out of their comfort zones while striving to improve their teaching in the classroom. Ms. D exemplified these traits. Her focus was never on herself but on her students; she was constantly willing to learn and grow to better serve her students at risk. Her willingness to implement the plans I helped her create was instrumental in helping me become more efficient and proficient in sharing this pedagogy.

Training others with the pedagogy on a broader scale occurred organically. While training Ms. D, I presented at several conferences, sharing the foundations of the pedagogy, my initial study, and the progress Ms. D and I were making with her students. At these conferences, teachers, professors and administrators inquired more and more about the pedagogy and opportunities for training. Realizing the opportunity to help educators, I selected a few of the schools as pilot sites for training in the pedagogy. As a result, I have provided training in a wide array of settings and with diverse groups of teachers and professors. In every case, the schools and educators I worked with were self-selected; they were not required to participate in my training. I have also streamlined the training process since working with Ms. D to the point that I can effectively teach small or large groups of educators during a few professional development days or in workshop settings.

The teachers and professors in my training sessions have come from a wide range of schools: traditional and alternative, rural and urban. They have also been extremely diverse demographically: men and women, different racial groups and ages, new and veteran teachers, and with varied levels of skill. Some teachers were extremely successful with the students in their classrooms; some faced great struggles in working with students at risk. What they all had in common, however, was a willingness to try something new and to move out of their comfort zone. They all selflessly admitted that they had room to grow as educators in the classroom.

Although each classroom situation is different and every class of students is unique, the practicality and beauty of this pedagogical model is that educators can adapt it to meet the diverse needs of any group of students in any subject area. All that is needed is the willingness of the educator to connect and to adapt and to believe that the students want to succeed, even when they don't know how to do so and seemingly sabotage their own efforts at every turn. Instructors of any subject can genuinely care for their students' success, relate to their students while viewing and treating them as equals, and dedicate time to understanding their students. We are the professionals. It is our task to meet our students' needs and to help them succeed. The Pedagogy of Real Talk can serve as another tool to help us achieve these goals.

# 9

## *The Training of Teachers*

The first section of this chapter is to suggest a potential structure or outline that educators can use when wanting to train others in the Pedagogy of Real Talk. Ultimately, it is up to the presenter to decide how he or she will do this, but I have found that this structure has worked well when beginning to teach educators how to use the approach. The first step is to determine which educators in a school or district are really interested in learning and implementing the approach. To do this, make an initial 45-minute presentation to the entire school faculty. In this presentation, introduce the pedagogy, show its success with the students, and give an overview of the outcomes. If possible, have a few teachers who have used the approach share their results and experiences. This allows more diversification and gives more teachers opportunities to share their experiences— teachers still "in the trenches" facing the same kinds of challenges as the teachers in the audience.

After the initial presentation, spend 30 to 60 minutes answering questions about the pedagogy and a series of related topics. Teachers typically ask questions of the teacher(s) who contributed to the presentation. End the presentation by announcing that you will return to begin the formal training but that their involvement will be strictly voluntary; they have absolutely no obligation or requirement to participate in the training. Immediately after the initial presentation, meet with administrators to create a schedule and to stress that they should not pressure any teachers to participate in the training.

The rationale behind not making the trainings mandatory is that teachers should have the autonomy to decide whether or not they wish to spend a minor amount of their time developing their teaching to better serve their students. In some cases, teachers genuinely do not have the time because of family obligations, graduate school, or second jobs to support their families. Often these teachers approach or email me to share their profound interest in the pedagogy and the reasons they cannot attend training at this time. Many of them ask their colleagues to share what they are learning, to keep them "up to speed." However, most teachers who choose not to attend are simply not interested. Working with a person or group of people who are forced to do something against their will is extremely complicated. They are uncooperative, unreceptive, resistant, and negative, and they often disengage from the group. By making participation in the training voluntary, you separate out the teachers who are not interested. However, because teaching is a highly personal craft, do not be offended when teachers are uninterested.

The teachers who volunteer for training of this sort are usually driven, open, and eager. They want to improve their teaching by learning and incorporating this alternative pedagogical approach. Always be open, welcoming, and as honest as possible with these teachers, and respect their time.

At the first official training session, spend time identifying teachers' strengths and areas for improvement. Ask teachers to self-reflect on their biggest classroom successes, challenges, and frustrations in working with their students. Responses tend to be fairly similar. For example, common themes regarding teachers' biggest challenges are (a) teaching students who are not motivated to learn or to do any work in their classrooms and (b) making learning interesting for students to generate an interest to learn. Frustrations shared by teachers usually include (a) not being able to earn the students' trust, to establish positive relationships with their students at risk, or to connect with their most challenging students; (b) dealing with a variety of negative attitudes (e.g., hostile, disrespectful, apathetic) in their classes; and (c) dealing with students' mood swings on a daily basis while attempting not to take them personally.

The most consistent and common forms of success teachers share are (a) connecting with their students and reaching them to teach them effectively and (b) seeing the results of their teaching through positive grades and test scores and changes in the attitude of the class. These are often the most valued forms of success for teachers working with students at risk. Unfortunately, teachers usually report that achieving that kind of success, especially on a consistent, large-scale, systematic level is rare. Connecting with students at risk, which is usually reported as a rare occurrence, is so important and meaningful that when teachers do succeed with their most challenging students, they consider it their biggest success. Interestingly, teachers are often able to identify and share various successes but cannot describe or verbalize the processes they used to achieve them.

Recognizing strengths is an important component of the training. Doing so allows teachers to capitalize on their strengths and to improve the areas in which they are struggling. The strengths of the teachers vary dramatically because they have so many diverse sets of strengths within their pedagogical approaches. One strength teachers often identify is being liked and respected by their students as a result of their teaching. Other strengths teachers often include are (a) strong, effective class structure; (b) a variety of exercises, lessons, homework, assignments, and readings that they use effectively throughout the academic year; and (c) their ability to get students to settle down, focus, and do their work. The highlight of this last strength is their ability to gain control of their classes in a manner that allows students who are interested in learning to learn. In other words, these teachers do not have classes that are completely out of control like those of other teachers. As teachers identify their strengths, they also explain their rationales for including them. Of note is that it is rare for teachers in training sessions to state that they have no areas that need improvement. Most are honest enough with themselves to acknowledge that they have gaps and want to fill those gaps to improve their teaching. You then identify the areas teachers hope to improve by implementing the Pedagogy of Real Talk.

You begin the formal portion of the training session by asking teachers to reflect once again on their biggest classroom challenge. Ask them to keep that as their reference point as you introduce the Pedagogy of Real Talk. Using this challenge, teachers begin to identify the ways in which the pedagogy may help them find new levels of success with their students at risk. As I mentioned earlier, the Pedagogy of Real Talk is something that can be used in its entirety or in segments. However, all teachers who participate in training sessions should be taught the entire approach. The teachers become familiar with all of the components and the ways in which they complement one another to make each more encompassing and successful in the classroom.

After the first official training session, try and observe the teachers in their classrooms. This helps to better understand their needs, the strengths and areas for improvement they shared, and the overall culture of the school. These observations are imperative to meet the needs of the teachers and the school most effectively. Because these needs vary from school to school, you cannot help teachers find applicable solutions if you do not take the time to get to know their classrooms and schools. Too often, outside experts come to schools for professional development days and present good ideas that are not very applicable to the specific needs of the schools. Observing teachers and spending a small amount of time in their schools allow you to customize the solutions offered through the Pedagogy of Real Talk.

# THE BASIC COMPONENTS AND
# FOUNDATIONS OF THE PEDAGOGY

The Pedagogy of Real Talk encompasses a variety of concepts that are equally important for success in applying the pedagogy. First, teachers must possess or be willing to attempt learning and implementing Meyer's characteristics of a successful teacher: (a) the ability to relate to students, (b) the ability to teach students, and (c) a genuinely positive attitude toward students. You can specifically address all three of Meyer's characteristics through group discussion and earnest, candid self-reflection concerning teachers' embodiment of these characteristics. For example, to help teachers and to ease this difficult process, I openly share my shortcomings within Meyer's characteristics when I first began teaching and how, in some cases, I still struggle with staying true to the characteristics. Also have the teachers accompanying you to present these trainings share the deficiencies within Meyer's characteristics they had before using the approach. Pedagogy is a highly personal craft. Therefore, in leading a workshop on teaching style, it is crucial to approach the topic in a sincere, open manner. Doing so commonly leads to the participants sharing the Meyer's characteristics they lack. Then work on identifying which characteristics they can strengthen within their approach to students.

Next, teachers must structure their classes using all of the S.C.R.E.A.M.+F variables to ensure they accommodate and integrate students' needs. Although students at risk may share a common stigmatizing label, they are very different individuals and are usually at risk of dropping out for a multitude of reasons, such as substance abuse and troubles at home. Having a classroom of students at risk means having a room of diverse individuals from diverse backgrounds who are in danger of failing for diverse reasons. Therefore, in implementing S.C.R.E.A.M.+F, teachers must remember the F, flexibility, to reinforce and emphasize the various components specifically needed by their students. Teachers must be willing to change based on the needs of their students rather than expecting their students to adjust to their instructors. Students may not be receptive to certain approaches. Instructors who can adjust their approaches will be more successful with these students. Thus, teachers must use S.C.R.E.A.M.+F as a flexible framework, developing it further as they adapt to their students.

Teachers can then approach their classes in a manner that engages both the teacher and students in learning simultaneously, as described by Freire. Through this mutual teaching and learning, students reveal components of their terministic screens. Once these revelations begin, teachers can use Real Talk discussions to capture the essence of each student and tie it into the academic curriculum, to establish powerful connections with students, or both. Teachers must remember, however, that the specific Real

Talks and terministic screens they identify for one group of students may not be appropriate for another group. Likewise, the insights teachers learn about one group of students from these components may not be applicable to another group. Therefore, teachers must be prepared to adjust as needed for each new group of students. Each class of students is different and should be treated that way. Where similarities and relevance between groups do exist, however, teachers should not hesitate to use the materials they have previously created.

## CONNECTIONS THROUGH REAL TALK

The second step of the training process involves defining Real Talk and providing examples of Real Talk discussions. Real Talk can be used in many different ways to improve the teaching and learning process. Its purpose is to establish connections, understanding, trust, empathy, and caring for one another between and among teachers and students in the classroom. Through Real Talk, teachers can also gain insight into students' terministic screens. This allows teachers to use Real Talk flexibly in their classrooms based on what they learn from their students. Ultimately, if we cannot establish connections with our students at risk, our lessons and whatever we are trying to teach them will fail, which, in turn, leads to our students being more resistant to the learning process.

Establishing Real Talk is essential during the first week of a course or class to begin building rapport and connections with students. With more experience, teachers may even integrate Real Talk discussions on the first day of class. Although these discussions are dependent on the students for their direct insight, teachers must initiate the steps in sharing to establish Real Talk in the classroom. One specific way to use Real Talk to build connections is to dismantle the negative stereotypes students may have of teachers because of their past experiences. Through Real Talk, teachers can more comfortably show the persons they are behind the position of teacher. Revealing appropriate personal information about ourselves through Real Talks is preferable to students assuming they have no connection to us. Teachers may think that their experiences are very different from those of their students, but this is rarely the case. By focusing Real Talks on universal themes (e.g., eagerness, happiness, frustration, motivation), teachers can overcome barriers and establish the similarities they share with their students as people. Through such Real Talks, teachers begin to establish powerful connections with their students as the students begin to see the teachers in front of them as persons rather than as generic teachers.

Teachers can also use Real Talks when students' morale is down, when students are not engaged or are frustrated, or to address anything that is inhibiting their students from focusing on the work they must complete in class. However, teachers must remember that Real Talk should not be used on a daily basis. Instead, teachers should incorporate Real Talks systematically yet genuinely in working with their students. As teachers master the use of Real Talk, they must use their discretion concerning how to best use this component in their classrooms.

Real Talks can also be used to help students connect to the material in the curriculum. In all subjects, teachers find particular chapters, concepts, or materials that are exceptionally difficult to teach because they do not generate student interest. Using Real Talk to introduce particularly challenging material often generates student eagerness or willingness to learn the material. Combined with alternative lessons, which we discuss in Chapter 10, Real Talk can increase students' receptivity to the material.

In developing Real Talk sessions, teachers must select themes that they can personalize from life experience to connect with students. The focus is not the exact experiences instructors share but the students' relationship to these universal themes. Using both positive and negative experiences creates broader connections with students, even when no direct similarities exist between the experiences of the students and those of their teachers. The entire process is based on a systematic approach to establish, strengthen, and solidify connections between teachers and students. Teachers can consistently use the understanding and relationships Real Talk generate to connect students to the material they must learn. Thus, teachers elevate students' genuine interest, engagement in class, and motivation to learn.

In this part of the training, teachers also have the opportunity to begin developing their own Real Talk topics. Each talk has a beginning, a middle, and an end. Teachers must use explicit transitions to guide and deliver these discussions. Creating a Real Talk requires seven steps, although the steps may vary from person to person. Thus, teachers should use these steps as a guide to begin a Real Talk and determine which steps are most useful to them:

1. Choose a theme and create your Real Talk outside of class.

2. Adjust your demeanor when delivering the Real Talk to captivate students, and begin with a leading question.

3. Begin your Real Talk broadly, define the universal theme, and then share your Real Talk.

4. Ask students if they have experienced this theme.

5. Ask students to share their examples of dealing with the theme.

6. Build connections between the various examples the students have shared.

7. End the Real Talk in one of two ways: Connect the Real Talk to what you are teaching that day or simply conclude the Real Talk with what you have shared.

Although this step-by-step breakdown of Real Talk may seem tedious or long-winded, in reality, the process flows naturally, concisely, and rhythmically.

## Step 1

Before any Real Talk is delivered with students, it must first be created outside of the class. As teachers become more experienced with Real Talk, they can create them instantaneously in class. First, teachers select a universal theme; within that theme, they must determine how they will share their particular experience or story with their students (see Appendix C). When first beginning to use Real Talk, teachers will expend both time and effort in the process. The story or experience exemplifying the chosen theme must make sense. The teacher must also be very careful not to use vernacular that is specific to the teacher but to use language that is easily understood by the students. Very often, teachers write out their Real Talks for review. I consistently find that, given their education, they write and want to deliver a Real Talk based on language that is easily understood by a college-educated audience. The problem is that our students do not necessarily use or understand the same language or the meanings of words in the same way as the teacher. Thus, many things that make sense to the teachers need to be described in a different manner for their students.

Once the Real Talks are written out, teachers need to practice them before conducting the actual Real Talks in their classrooms. Practice is not intended to create a formal presentation or an over-rehearsed delivery of a speech. Instead, it is to help teachers feel comfortable, and be succinct and purposeful (while maintaining authenticity) with the delivery of a Real Talk. Too often, we witness people with powerful messages or meaningful things to share but with weak or seemingly scattered delivery. This makes it difficult for the intended audience to follow the message and causes the audience to disengage from what is being said. Practicing allows teachers to trust themselves and to resist deviating from their intended purpose in delivering a Real Talk. However, I must stress that this practice is not about preparing a keynote speech, workshop or class presentation, or formal speech. Here, practice allows teachers to identify areas for improvement to enhance the quality of their Real Talks further in the hope of building connectedness with their students.

## Step 2

Delivering the Real Talk in the classroom begins with the teacher changing his or her demeanor and the selection of the questions that the teacher will ask surrounding the identified universal theme. By *change demeanor*, I mean teachers must purposely change the manner in which they stand in front of the class, their tone of voice, the extent to which they show emotion, and any other physical and verbal actions they commonly use when working with their students. Teachers must be very specific and evident as they immediately prepare to ask their students their leading question. The teacher's demeanor should be one of mixed emotions. For example, the teacher's voice should have a slightly more serious tone without being authoritative, a tone showing the teacher is both earnest and vulnerable. However, within that vulnerability, teachers must remain in control of emotions. Too much emotion will disconnect the students from what the teacher is trying to relay. This change in demeanor will also help students sense that their teachers are going to deliver something different from the usual lecture or discussion.

On changing demeanor, the teacher's first interaction using Real Talk with students is to ask a question embedded with the universal theme. This is the initial hook when beginning a Real Talk. For example, a teacher asked her students, "Does anyone know what rejection means?" Or another example, "Has anyone in class ever felt angry because they were so frustrated?" The question is not one that is necessarily meant to be answered; rather, it is more rhetorical in nature. Although teachers will notice that the question will grab the attention of the students as it is meant to, they should not wait for students to answer the question literally. Its purpose is to attract their attention. Teachers may hear some students make comments in agreement with the question or physically show their agreement. Once teachers have asked the question and have their students' attention, teachers should immediately delve into the Real Talk.

Worth noting is that as you progress and improve on your usage of Real Talk, it will not always be necessary to pose a question to your students. For example, as you improve, you can start by making a statement followed by your personal experience or whatever you decide to share with your students. Another method is to use visuals of something that is personal to you and begin to share your experience surrounding the image you are showing. Regardless of how you begin, you should always hook students. You should also keep a universal theme within all Real Talks, whether explicit or implicit. The more you do Real Talk, the more comfortable and better you will get at using it and making the necessary adjustments that best fit your needs.

## Step 3

The teacher begins by talking about what his or her chosen universal theme (e.g., adversity, gratefulness, frustration) means in general, providing a clear definition for students. By beginning broadly, the instructor can funnel the talk into a more detailed, meaningful discussion about a direct experience that begins to connect students to the theme. The first connection occurs when the teacher shares a personal experience with the theme. It is optimal and preferable for teachers to share their own authentic experiences. However, teachers can authentically apply or share the experiences of others with whom they are close, such as friends and family, or use biographies, events, or experiences based on popular culture or media. The point of the teacher sharing these experiences is to deepen the connection between understanding the theme and the reality of experiencing the theme. This also allows the students to see teachers as persons beyond their positions in the classroom.

## Step 4

Teachers should then ask the students if they have experienced or know someone who has experienced the theme. By asking if they know someone who has experienced the theme, it allows students who are not comfortable sharing about themselves an opportunity to contribute comfortably. The wording of this request should be an explicit transition from teacher to students. It is not essential that students confirm their experiences with the theme by raising their hands. Any form of agreement (e.g., verbal comments, physically nodding their heads, attentive or positive changes in the atmosphere) is sufficient to acknowledge the students' involvement. When teachers first begin using Real Talk, they may not receive overwhelming response from their classes. This is often because the students are surprised by what their teachers are doing; they are not accustomed to teachers engaging them and sharing in this manner. Teachers will normally notice changes in the demeanor of their classes as the students listen to the Real Talk. Slowly but surely, some students will acknowledge what their teachers are sharing; others may talk with their teachers after class to share the impact of the Real Talk in private. A clear indicator that students are focused on the Real Talk is the pin drop phenomenon: having a classroom filled with students at risk so intensely focused on every word their teacher is saying that one can hear a pin drop. The time between asking the question and observing students' responses should be very short. Teachers should also follow this step immediately with Step 5.

## Step 5

Teachers should ask students to share any specific examples of dealing with the theme. The sharing can be their own personal examples or examples of someone they know. This should be a strictly voluntary activity. In the first Real Talk in a class, few students will volunteer, although typically at least two or three students offer specific examples. As students share, teachers should be active listeners, remaining reassuring and receptive while listening intently to every word their students are saying. Teachers may also need to help students verbalize their thoughts. Many students are not used to sharing their personal thoughts and may struggle to communicate them verbally. Teachers should help them clarify their explanations and encourage them to help them feel more comfortable.

As students share, the other students commonly listen intently. The atmosphere of the classroom begins to shift as the people within it begin to relate to each other rather than remain a group of disconnected individuals. After each student who wishes to do so shares experiences or insights, teachers should reiterate the connection of those experiences to the theme. Then proceed to Step 6.

In the event that students do not share, teachers should not assume that the Real Talk was a failure. Teachers must remember to pay close attention to their students throughout the Real Talk. If the students are captivated, completely focused, or engaged with the teacher, that means that the Real Talk is affecting the students. If they do not respond, teachers should proceed to Step 7 to conclude the Real Talk.

## Step 6

Teachers should build connections between what the students have shared. Using universal themes, teachers can begin to dismantle differences and highlight similarities. To do this, teachers must show the variations of the theme nearly all people experience and how each student who shared brought one of those variations to light. This method helps students feel empowered in the class, showing them that they are contributing to the overall experience and knowledge of the class.

By helping the class begin to feel empowered, teachers also highlight the commonalities they share through their diverse experiences, which begins to establish the classroom as a safe place to be open and accepting of one another. This step can also affect attendance positively, solidifying the classroom as a place where students feel stability and the freedom to be themselves. Real Talk can transform the classroom into a place where the turmoil many students at risk typically face within their lives is absent. They do not have to worry about the many things within their lives that add stress, albeit perhaps only for the hour they spend in class.

## Step 7

The final step is another transition that concludes the Real Talk. Once teachers garner insight from their students and their experiences, they must connect the Real Talk to what they are teaching in class. If that is not possible, or if the original intent of the Real Talk is not specific to the curriculum, teachers should connect the Real Talk with their students. Teachers may also attempt to do both. For example, in the Real Talk described in Appendix C, the teacher connects adversity to both establishing connections with others and to the curriculum. The teacher shows the students that by passing the class, they are overcoming a form of adversity that the class poses for some students. The students recognize adversity within their own lives and eventually understand that the challenge the curriculum represents for them is a form of adversity that they are facing within their lives. For a plethora of reasons (e.g., lack of effort, lack of understanding, intimidation, personal or family responsibilities), achieving success in school is a big challenge for this population of students, a form of adversity for many of them. Through Real Talk, the teacher identifies that all people share the experience of some form of adversity and, as a result, attempts to bring the class together. Through this Real Talk, the teacher helps students turn the curriculum from an oppositional force that will "beat them" into an obstacle they can overcome by successfully preparing through the work they do in class. Ultimately, the teacher and students work together toward a common goal instead of working against one another in the classroom. Lastly, end every Real Talk on some sort of positive note and not on a negative one.

## ANOTHER REAL TALK EXAMPLE

As we have discussed previously, giving students a voice in class by incorporating their perspectives and experiences is very important in engaging them with the learning process. More important is the teacher's ability to connect with students and to help connect students' perspectives to the academic curriculum to ensure they meet the final academic goals for the course. As teachers discover the students' terministic screens, they must create or adjust Real Talks and lessons based on this information. In doing so, however, teachers must maintain the integrity of the material, not "water it down." In this section, I show how I connected the focus of adversity to the specific reading and writing curricula over the course of three separate days. The Real Talk led to the creation of alternative lessons. Ultimately, although these lessons grew from the Real Talk, they were not dependent on it. The assignments should reveal how resourceful, beneficial, and diverse Real Talks can be.

### Day 1

Students in writing class completed in-class exercises in their textbooks, which students had been assigned to read as homework the night before. These exercises reinforced the concepts of paragraph structure, topic sentences, and transitions. The students began this process by discussing the different types of adversity they had overcome within their lives or current adversities they were trying to overcome. Students were divided into groups of four to do this assignment. Usually dividing groups of students at risk can be challenging. Most struggle to work independently; adding the group dynamic increases this struggle. In this case, the Real Talk had nullified the negative aspects of group work sufficiently so that students could openly discuss their issues with adversity.

After a few minutes of group discussion, students transitioned into writing their experiences, following the rules for writing that they needed to learn. Each student had to write a few paragraphs regarding the form of adversity they had shared with their group.

Once they completed their writing, the groups exchanged papers immediately to begin the process of editing. They began with a paper from a student who volunteered to have the class edit the paper. The paper was projected so that the class could follow along. In the editing process, we addressed topic sentences, paragraph structure, and transitions. After we went over this paper together, students were asked to review their papers to see if they noticed things they needed to improve to meet the writing standards they needed to learn. Some individuals who were quicker at grasping the concepts than others volunteered to help those who were further behind to understand the material.

After they completed editing their work, we had a brief discussion as a class on what they had learned, what had been easy to understand, and what had been difficult. This ending discussion helped solidify what students understood, which students needed further development in specific areas, and whether the students were ultimately learning the material.

## Day 2

Students in writing class began a Real Talk discussion on failing when faced with adversity. They began the class by sharing that the Real Talk we had had a few days earlier made them reflect on many things within their lives. This Real Talk was led by a group of five students. This group shared how they had all talked about their similarities regarding their concern about going back home a failure. Successful completion of school was their challenge, but they realized that their biggest fear was to go back home and tell everyone that they had failed. An overwhelming number of students in class agreed with this assessment as they shared how much love and support they had received from specific people within their lives and how proud those people were of them for simply being accepted into the program. Their fear was failure in the face of adversity, not for themselves but for those who believed in them, because so few people within their lives had ever believed in them.

A few students spoke up and said they had no one back home or anyone in their lives, so they had to overcome this challenge on their own with no support. Nonetheless, they still feared failing. When the students shared about not having support within their lives, many other students in class responded directly to them, telling them they now had the full support of their fellow classmates who respected them and believed in them. This turn in the discussion unfolded on its own, led by the students. The impact of Real Talk was profound on these students, and even more so that the students took initiative and supported one another. The momentum of this heightened mood and focus worked well to transition back to the curriculum.

The student's focus was redirected to the curriculum (topic sentences) in their text. The class was asked to define and explain topic sentences and to generate a topic sentence for a paragraph about fear of failing when faced with adversity. Using their Real Talk experiences, several students provided examples of topic sentences. All the students then had five minutes to create topic sentences based on their individual experiences.

Next, students were separated into small groups. Within each group, students chose one of the experiences their members had shared during their Real Talk. They then created an introductory paragraph using a topic sentence based on the experience they selected. As each group read its paragraph out loud, the class identified the topic sentence within the paragraph.

Next, the groups created three to five possible transitions to link the introductory paragraph with the next paragraph they needed to create. Each group shared these sample transitions verbally and visually by writing them on the chalkboard.

Finally, students wrote essays regarding fear of failing when faced with adversity. Students were reminded to use transitions and to have clear topic sentences. Whatever work they did not finish in class was homework to be turned in the next day.

## Day 3

In reading class, interpreting symbols and images was used from the curriculum in the reading textbook and connected to the Real Talk discussion on adversity. Students were asked if any of them knew what a symbol was. After defining the term and giving examples, the students shared symbols within their lives that represented adversity to them. One student shared that before coming to the program, teachers symbolized adversity for her because throughout her entire life, she had constantly had issues with teachers. Another student explained how police officers were a symbol of adversity, even oppression, in the area in which he grew up. Another student shared how drugs were a symbol of adversity for him because he had struggled with drug addiction throughout his life. As students shared their examples, we began to transition to the curriculum. We continued with a discussion of the importance of symbols in reading passages and written works. Students then read a series of short excerpts from a variety of texts, extracted the symbols, and determined what they meant within what they had read.

With this particular Real Talk, the focus was establishing connections with students and tying it into the class work students had to do. I could have simply focused on connecting with students. As discussed previously, Real Talk is flexible. Teachers must use their discretion to determine whether to focus Real Talk on connections, curriculum, or both. That decision must be based on what the class needs from the Real Talk.

In the appendices, there are diverse sets of examples to help teachers see the different ways in which they can use Real Talk. It is a systematic way to establish successful and consistent connections with students on multiple levels in the classroom to help them succeed. Instead of being a one-dimensional approach, Real Talk has been purposefully designed to reinvigorate and motivate students and teachers.

It is through establishing connections with students at risk that we begin the process of building their receptiveness to learning the material they must comprehend to succeed in school. Real Talk allows this to happen successfully throughout the semester in a deliberate yet authentic manner. Through Real Talk, teachers gain insight and understanding into students' terministic screens; it is the most effective and reliable approach within the pedagogy to do so. As teachers use these discussions strategically throughout the semester, students reveal the person behind the student every time. Real Talk effects and solidifies the connections between teachers and students at risk. However, because Real Talks are such powerful tools, teachers should not use them every day. Instead, to sustain connections and relationships with students, teachers should use the information in the following chapter to supplement Real Talks.

## MAINTAINING CONNECTIONS

Regardless of students' backgrounds, teachers can find connections to make their learning meaningful to students through Freire's dialogue, active listening, and engaging students to share their thoughts and perspectives. By approaching students in this alternative manner, you can break through their first line of defense in resisting teachers. Students begin to see teachers more positively, not seeing them as stereotypes or oppositional forces. Establishing a positive relationship with students results in better academic performance and fewer problems in school compared with the performance and problems of students who have more negative views of teachers and school.

Relating to students is a matter not merely of having some similarities with students but of "developing a rapport with them, talking with them, laughing with them, counseling them, reaching them on their own level."[1] Sharing a similar background with students does not guarantee success in teaching them. Students have to first view and acknowledge teachers as people, not just as teachers. Many students at risk view teachers as entities that only exist within the classroom; they do not exist in the real world. Because of this view, these students stigmatize teachers further by believing their understanding and knowledge base exists only within the classroom. Thus, they create a barrier for teachers attempting to connect with their

---

[1]See Hernandez, "College 101: Introducing At-Risk Students to Higher Education," 2.

students. To dismantle this barrier and build connections with students, teachers must be authentic. They must listen to their students without judgment. As discussed earlier, every human feels frustration, ostracism, insecurity, betrayal, joy, accomplishment, and a host of other universal themes. Teachers must find each student's connection point through a universal theme, event, feeling, or experience.

When teachers allow students insight into some personal aspects of their lives, they also help build rapport and engage students. Share your personal experiences with students; borrow stories from friends and family; and use themes from current news, events, or biographies. Some people may not be as comfortable as others in revealing personal information to their students. Therefore, instructors must determine their own comfort levels in answering any personal questions their students pose. In addition, teachers must always be sure that what they choose to share is appropriate for their students. It takes time and skill to develop the appropriate mixture of sharing and maintaining one's position of authority in the classroom.

To do this, teachers should take small steps, sharing information that does not make them feel uncomfortable or vulnerable rather than being an "open book" and divulging massive amounts of personal information. Start with something simple, like telling the class about a pet. Expand on what this pet means to you, what you enjoy about your pet, and what things your pet does that you find annoying, funny, or strange. A teacher that was not very comfortable with sharing anything personal with his students took a different route. He feared that they would use it against him or, even worse, that they would judge him. He began small, simply asking the class, "How many of you have a pet at home?" After many of his students raised their hands, he shared that he had no pets. Some of his students asked why he had no pets, and the process of sharing information continued. He did not feel threatened or pressured during this exchange and began in earnest the process of connecting with his students.

Another teacher struggled to open up to students because she was worried that whatever she shared would be used against her in class. Rather than start with information that was too private, she began with something about her that usually surprises people who think they know her. She explained that most people thought she had never done anything wrong or tried anything drastic in her life. However, she had been a heavy cigarette smoker in college, which always surprised people who thought they knew her. She was not embarrassed about being a former smoker. In fact, she was very proud that she had overcome the addiction. She decided to share this with her students through playing a game of two truths and one lie to make the process lighthearted and fun. After trying this game, she shared the outcome with her students. Her excitement was exhilarating. She reported that everything had gone extremely well. Her students were shocked that she had once been addicted to cigarettes. In fact, the game had sparked conversation and interest from her students, things she was not accustomed to but which she enjoyed very much. She had not done a formal Real Talk by any means, but simply by sharing authentically, she had begun to establish connections with her students.

Such personal information may seem trivial at first. In reality, sharing such simple information can be a powerful beginning to breaking down barriers between teachers and students at risk by highlighting the commonalities between teachers and students. Once sharing is established, teachers can continue to share to increase their comfort level, gaining confidence in the process and building connections with their students.

By applying the strategies of this pedagogy and adapting them to their own personal style, teachers can create connections and relate to students in a variety of settings. Regardless of backgrounds or beliefs, by engaging students with real-life experiences in open settings and allowing students to get to know them as people, not just as teachers, instructors can break down walls and develop constructive relationships. These relationships will, in turn, provide the foundations for successful teaching and learning.

# 10

## *Training: Alternative Lessons*

Teachers must then relate whatever subjects are important in their students' lives to the curricular material, formulating lessons and discussions to reach out to those characteristics. It is crucial to maintain interconnectedness between each lesson and the core academic concepts. Although creating unique classroom lessons is not a new concept, engaging an entire class of learners at risk is extraordinary. By applying the fundamental concepts of the Pedagogy of Real Talk, practically any lesson can entice students to be involved and establish receptiveness to learning from their teachers if it is based on students' terministic screens. Teachers will rely on these alternative lessons daily throughout their courses. They are crucial in sustaining student engagement, eagerness, and dedication to learning in between the strategically placed Real Talks. Thus, alternative lessons are a wonderful complement to Real Talk and the connections established with students in the classroom.

As we defined earlier, alternative lessons combine the content standard(s) from the curriculum with either the terministic screens of the students or societal issues outside of the classroom that will connect with students' terministic screens or resonate with them on a personal level. Through the creation and implementation of these lessons, teachers can create more encompassing connections to class material and sustain and complement the connections they have made with Real Talk. Using a step-by-step guide in this chapter and three examples from different teachers that show their alternative lessons, teachers should be able to create their own. The appendices also contain several alternative lessons created by other teachers.

Any time we are delivering lessons to our students, we run the risk of alienating them as we can easily fall into the trap of talking at the class and causing students to become disengaged from what we are attempting to teach them. Additionally, we also face the challenge that students do not see the material we are attempting to teach them as relevant; in some cases, students are simply intimidated by the seemingly complex material they must learn. These are common and everyday scenarios within classrooms in all educational institutions. But through alternative lessons, we are able to effectively overcome these barriers.

The process in creating an alternative lesson is simple but not simplistic and, as with Real Talk, I am offering the steps as a guide. Ultimately educators will decide what steps are most useful for them.

1. Analyze the concept(s) you must teach your students.

2. Determine how the concept(s) can be connected to students' terministic screens or real-life situations.

3. Begin a comprehensive search for visuals, video clips, unique articles, pictures, and so on. If you do not use visual aids, be sure to pose clear scenarios and questions to students.

4. Piece together all the information to create an alternative lesson around the concept(s) or standard(s) students must learn.

5. Determine how you will assess student learning and determine effectiveness of the lesson.

6. Use your alternative lesson with your students.

## Step 1

Begin by analyzing the concept or standard that the students must learn. By this, I mean that we cannot take for granted that we know the material we must teach our students. We must assess our own understanding of what we must teach our students critically to clearly see how to begin to creatively connect the material with our students. Additionally, in some cases, we are tasked to teach subjects that we are not so familiar with. Whether it's a new class, a class we have not taught in a long time, or something we are simply not well versed in—whatever the reason, these types of situations require our attention to make sure we analyze all the concepts we must teach our students. Our in-depth understanding of what we must teach will better serve our teaching the material to students.

## Step 2

You cannot build or create an alternative lesson until you view the curriculum content and find a way to fuse the material with the students' terministic screens, what you have learned about them overall, or real-life events that will resonate with them. You can do this by reflecting on what you have learned about your students through Real Talks, dialogue, and all the other techniques used to gain insight into students. Also, you can use yourself and your life experiences when you feel that you do not have enough information gathered from students' terministic screens or experiences. This step is a reflection of what you have learned about your students. For new classes whose students you have not yet met you must rely on real-life events that are in the media, popular culture, or anything else that will help you bring to life the concepts you are attempting to teach your students. Rather than ignore what is happening beyond the concrete walls of your classroom, bring the outside world into the classroom and connect it to what they must learn.

## Step 3

In this step, you should simply conduct a search on the Internet or perhaps sort through books, articles, newspapers, and so on, to find the appropriate material that you would like to use within your alternative lesson. Take your time to do a comprehensive search. This will lead you to find as much relevant material as possible, but it will also allow you to make sure you are using credible and appropriate material. Once you have collected the material you will use for your alternative lesson, you move on to the next step.

## Step 4

At this point, you have collected all of the different material you have decided on using. Now you combine everything to create the alternative lesson. You fuse the concept or standard, terministic screens of your students or real-life events, and the material you decided to use from your search. You have now created an alternative lesson.

## Step 5

Before you deliver an alternative lesson, you must determine what rubric you will use or create to assess student learning in your classroom. This step is specific to the needs of each individual teacher and the manner in which they are asked to assess their students' progress. Assessing the success of your students through the alternative lesson is crucial to successfully show the growth that they have experienced.

Some examples are teachers who distribute a quiz, a test, writing assignment, or any other type of assignment to measure how well students learned and understood the concept(s) or standards within the alternative lesson. In other cases, teachers simply give a cumulative exam or project that students must complete after several days or weeks of the teacher having used alternative lessons. Ultimately, you should use whatever best serves you, your students, and the school's needs.

## Step 6

After having completed the steps to create an alternative lesson, you are now ready to deliver it in your classroom. Remember to keep a few things in mind regarding an alternative lesson. Be creative and do not restrict yourself, but use discretion as you create these lessons. Alternative lessons are about not simply the creation but also the delivery. Alternative lessons can begin seemingly far removed from the content that students must learn, but eventually they connect directly to what students must learn in class. There is also no specific length of time that you should adhere to. They can be 10, 15, 20, or 30 minutes long, and in some cases, they can even be delivered over the course of days or weeks. If students find the material relevant, are engaged, and feel connected to the teacher, they will be far more receptive to learning and in turn become more successful in school compared to when these components are missing in the teacher–student relationship.

# ALTERNATIVE LESSON EXAMPLES

In this section, I have added examples from three teachers who are in different subjects and created their own alternative lessons. The diversity among alternative lessons should be clear in this section, along with the uniqueness of each one. But overall, they all share the foundation required to create alternative lessons. The manner in which each teacher begins and delivers the alternative lesson varies, but they all have shared that their students were receptive and engaged, learned the necessary material effectively, and did not demonstrate the typical resistance they were historically known to offer.

## U.S. History: Discrimination

The following example shows how a teacher created an alternative lesson for her U.S. history class. She began the process by brainstorming what she had learned about her students through Real Talk. She identified a list of things she had learned that she could potentially fuse with the unit on the Civil Rights Movement: discrimination, prejudice, unequal treatment, and bias. She eventually selected unequal treatment as the starting point and began to find ways to connect it to the students' terministic screens and eventually to the Civil Rights Movement.

She then used the Internet to gather additional ideas. She was careful with the information she gathered, ensuring that it was from reliable sources. In addition to Internet sources (e.g., YouTube clips, pictures, media articles, academic journal articles), she searched in books, articles, autobiographies, photographs, and anything else she found compelling.

After all of her searching, this teacher used a test she had in her collection of resources from a 1996 edition of *Social Education*. The article included a lesson teachers could use in their social studies classes on the injustice of the Alabama literacy tests created in the 1960s to disenfranchise the African American population.[1] The test was one of the actual exams administered to potential voters in Alabama during that time and had been purposely created to be nearly impossible for African Americans to pass, thus keeping them from voting. Her objective was to help students understand and feel in a small way the frustration and injustice of these tests.

She used this existing lesson but put her own spin on it by making subtle changes to bring her students' terministic screens to the forefront of the lesson. She did not focus on voting as the original lesson did but rather on test taking. She knew her students had a negative perspective on tests and disliked them for a multitude of reasons. Thus, although she used an existing resource as the framework, she took the lesson in a different direction to create her own alternative lesson.

When she began the lesson, she first tapped into her students' terministic screens by having them write a response to this prompt: "Think of a time when you were treated unfairly, and explain what happened." Starting the lesson in this manner allowed students to reveal their terministic screens as they wrote about being treated unfairly. She then moved to the next step in her lesson. As her students were writing, she abruptly stopped them and announced, "Oh! I forgot you have a test we need to take. So put your answers aside for now and get ready for the test." Her students were shocked by the statement because they had taken a unit test the previous day. Her students responded with typical resistance, ranging from passive aggressiveness, anger, and frustration to challenging her rationale for having to take another test. She simply said, "Just take the exam because we have talked about this, so you should know it." She also let them know that if they did not take the test, she might lower their grade by an entire letter grade. This forcefully encouraged students to take the test. Even though the students took the exam, she still encountered some resistance from students who vocalized their discontent: "This is not fair."

---

[1] "1965 Alabama Literacy Test," *Social Education* 60, no. 6 (1996): 340.

She then added to their being upset by announcing that they had only 20 minutes to complete the exam, which consisted of 60 questions.

At the end of the time limit, she collected the tests and announced that she would let them know by the end of the day what they had scored. As she tried to move on to another topic, her students immediately resisted her, not allowing her to teach as they continued to speak about how upset they were about the impromptu test. Not letting things get out of control, she moved to the next part of her alternative lesson and immediately addressed the test: "It is a fake test. It will not count." Her students immediately made the connection to the writing prompt she had initiated earlier when she smiled and asked, "So what did I just do to all of you?" Her students shared that they felt they were being discriminated against because they were students who were at the mercy of the teacher. They felt helpless in being forced to do something they felt was unfair.

She then asked, "How did it feel to be treated unfairly by someone who has more power than you in a particular setting?" This led to intense dialogue regarding the topic of being treated unfairly, which she connected to discrimination in society. Having an open, receptive, and amicable discussion on discrimination was not a common occurrence in her class. This topic in her course was usually very challenging because many of the students resisted acknowledging societal disparities between racial groups. Some of her students were not interested because they viewed racial discrimination as a thing of the past; others simply shut down because they did not want to discuss the topic. Her students came from a rural area, and her class overwhelmingly consisted of one racial group, thus little racial diversity existed. Although I cannot determine if her students were racially biased or not based on the information she shared, the topic of race was challenging for them as it is for many students, teachers, and people within the United States. Through this alternative lesson, the teacher helped her students become receptive to the unit on the Civil Rights Movement by bringing discrimination to the forefront of her students' minds.

Although many of her students connected the content to themselves, teachers cannot simply assume that students will make connections to their own lives. Teachers must always be prepared to guide students if they need help to make the connections. In this case, the teacher asked her students how they personally felt about the unfair test and guided those who struggled to make the connection immediately.

Ultimately, this alternative lesson was extremely powerful. It struck a chord with students because they felt powerlessness, isolation, and unequal treatment within their own lives. The students realized that what was being asked of them in their class and what they needed to comprehend were actually connected to larger societal issues. The key was to show them the connection between what they were learning and their own terministic screens, personal experiences, and material that resonated with them on a personal level. Her alternative lesson took about 30 minutes, but as the teacher shared, "It made a personal connection and resonated with them, leaving a lasting impression, and led to their receptiveness of the Civil Rights Movement unit."

## Mathematics: Building Bridges

A math teacher in an inner-city school considered to be one of the lowest performing schools within its state and the country openly shared her challenges. She shared that her school was extraordinarily challenging for her as a first-year teacher. Culturally, she struggled as a middle class European American teacher in a predominantly African American, poverty-stricken community. She also shared that her administration was not supportive, and that her students were not interested in what was being taught in her classrooms. However, this teacher was extraordinarily dedicated to her students and was determined. As she was trained and developed in the Pedagogy of Real Talk, she showed she was very talented in creating alternative lessons for a subject matter that students struggled with tremendously.

Through a Real Talk she learned that her students were interested in being recognized and acknowledged for having accomplished something significant within their lives. Although this may seem trivial to some, this was a major breakthrough for any teacher in her school as there were no other teachers who were able to gather this type of personal insight from her students. She used the information she learned from her students by creating an alternative lesson. This alternative lesson is what helped her overcome the challenge of teaching a geometry class to students who were simply not interested in learning anything about the subject.

She decided to focus on center of mass and gravity, symmetry and the power of triangles, and stability for her alternative lesson. She knew the concepts very well and decided that the best way to connect them to her students was to have them build something in her class. She searched the Internet and focused on YouTube videos to show her class. The first set of videos she decided to use was of different bridges collapsing; the next video was a news report of people "planking"[2] (lying face down with hands touching the sides of the body, sometimes in an unusual location). Last, she showed students how to use an interactive website to build shapes.[3]

After having conducted her search, she decided to use the videos of bridges collapsing as her initial "hook" to generate students' interest in her alternative lesson. After this, she would ask her students if they were interested in breaking a world record. Her focus was to have student teams build bridges out of Popsicle sticks and to see how much weight the bridges could withstand before they broke. She would follow this by sharing

---

[2]https://www.youtube.com/watch?v=tRHnTFesv7c

[3]http://www.mathsisfun.com/geometry/symmetry-artist.html

that their goal was to set a world record by competing against one another with the bridges they built. Her alternative lesson became multiple alternative lessons with the ultimate goal of reaching the final lesson of having them build their bridges. But before building bridges, students had to learn the concepts involved in building a bridge. This meant that they would have to learn about center of mass and gravity, symmetry and the power of triangles, and stability.

She separated each of the concepts into what she called mini lessons. This whole process happened over the course of five school days: The mini lessons were conducted over the course of two days, the building of the bridges took two days, and the weight test was conducted on the fifth day. Every mini lesson students had to do was clearly connected to the ultimate goal of building their bridge and establishing a world record. She also had rubrics built into the lessons to determine if the students were learning the material for her geometry class.

When she felt ready to deliver her alternative lesson, she did so by first asking her students if they had ever witnessed a bridge collapse. As she asked her question, she had her videos ready to show the class. As she showed the videos, her students were instantaneously engaged as they laughed and expressed amazement at the videos. (Like many other students at risk, her students would laugh at things that were generally considered more serious than humorous in nature.) She used their engagement as the opportunity to ask them the question whether they were interested in breaking a world record by building a bridge made out of Popsicle sticks that could withstand an enormous amount of weight. Her students responded with excitement and eagerness. She shared with the class that they would first have to learn what it takes to build a strong bridge, and as soon they were done learning this, they would apply what they learned by building their own bridges. Her students agreed and were ready for what they needed to learn.

Her first mini lesson focused on center of mass and gravity. Before beginning the lesson she showed students a short news report on planking to begin the discussion and work on center of mass and gravity. Her students were intrigued by the video, as it was a current fad within popular culture, and students knew about it. After a brief discussion, she moved on to the next part of the lesson. She had a series of objects for students to interact with and asked the students to find the center of mass for each. She kept them engaged by having them work with their hands, but also kept them interested and prevented them from becoming frustrated, as they were eager to get to the larger goal of building their bridges. Additionally, she also had students become involved physically by having them use their bodies in the process of attempting to figure out their own center of mass and gravity. Lastly, she had students determine stability by exploring various building/bridge designs and examined 3D shapes to determine how buildings/bridges become stable. (See Appendix J for all of her mini lessons.)

Her second mini lesson was on symmetry and the power of the triangle. Before she had her students begin their work, she reminded them again of the importance of the work they would be doing today in making sure they would build strong bridges that could withstand large amounts of weight. As she began the work, her first step was having students go to the Math Is Fun website[4] to use something interactive to design symmetric shapes. Once they created the shapes, she had students explain why symmetry is important to a bridge. Additionally, she had them explore why triangles are important to building bridges and other structures. She had students build different shapes with card stock and fasteners that included shapes with triangles and without triangles, and students applied force to the shapes to determine the weakest points. Ultimately, students connected everything they learned back to their bridges, as their next step was now to begin their process of building their bridge.

She had her students do something that was also unusual and difficult within her school. She had students work in groups as they began building their bridges. Working in groups was not common in her school. Students struggled to work independently, and to work in groups usually meant chaos or even fights among students. But in this case, the teacher had absolutely no problems with her students working together. In fact, they worked so well together and she was so proud of them that she took pictures of her students while they worked in teams to design and build their bridges. The final steps students took were designing their bridges in their groups; creating a "college report" that included their objective, materials, hypothesis, and procedure; their calculations of how many Popsicle sticks they would need; their analysis, conclusion, and revision and reflection; and lastly their peer-to-peer evaluation. Although this process may seem tedious on paper, it took little time to create but paid dividends within her classroom.

On the day students finished building their bridges and the competition began, involvement went well beyond engaging that one class in the alternative lesson. Her students had been so excited and proud that they'd discussed what they were doing in her class with many other students and teachers in the school. Students from other classes asked their teachers' permission to witness the bridges being tested, and many were allowed to attend. As the teams began putting weights on their bridges, one bridge at a time until they finally broke, they were cheered on and encouraged by the audience that had filled her classroom to be a part of this day. Not only were her own students engaged from beginning to end, but students from other classes also asked to be in her class to do similar types of assignments. Visitors learned an enormous amount of information that they needed for their geometry class, but they had fun, were engaged, saw the work as relevant, and were invested in their

---

[4]http://www.mathsisfun.com/geometry/symmetry-artist.html

learning process. The bridge that ultimately won the competition was able to withstand 145 pounds; they ran out of weights to further test the bridge, and it did not break.

The math teacher's alternative lesson varies tremendously from the history teacher's lesson and you will notice the same for the Spanish teacher's alternative lesson in the final example.


## Spanish: Stereotypes

The Spanish teacher worked in an inner-city school that was almost 100% African American within a community steeped in poverty. His school was considered low performing, where less than 60% of students graduated from high school. He also initially struggled to connect with his students; as a middle-class European American teacher, he admittedly found it difficult to connect with his students, who seemed so different from him. As he progressed in his semester, he slowly but surely began to connect with his students through Real Talk and other methods he found useful in his class. As he connected with his students, he still faced a difficult challenge. His students admittedly shared with him that they had no interest in Spanish; in fact, they did not appreciate having to learn it because they saw no use for it. The Spanish teacher was in part able to overcome this with a combination of alternative lessons and through the connection he made with his students to teach them the relevancy of being at the very least bilingual in the global society that we live in. But his first step was generating an interest in what he was teaching in class.

Ultimately, the Spanish teacher was tasked to teach students how to understand and speak basic Spanish. But he also felt it was important for students to understand the cultural diversity and individual cultures found within the Spanish-speaking countries. This led to one of his first alternative lessons, focusing on the unit that needed to be covered on clothing, but he also decided to teach students about the diversity among Latinos beyond the stereotypical views some people have within the United States.

As he assessed what he had to teach them and felt comfortable in his understanding of it, he immediately began to think of his students' terministic screens. He knew that his students struggled with being young African Americans who are stereotyped within society. He embedded this insight into his alternative lesson. He then moved on and began his search on the Internet to look for images he would use in his alternative lesson. As he searched, he decided that he would highlight the diversity in phenotypes among Latinos. As he picked the different people he would use, he decided to use images of them in different styles of dress such as professional and casual attire. He also decided to pick different Spanish magazines that he would bring to class to have students work with as well. Once he had all of this information, he was able to put it together to create his alternative lesson. He ultimately brought all of his material together through a PowerPoint to show the visuals and present his alternative lesson to his class. Lastly, his method of assessing students was to have them speak in Spanish to one another on the subject matter and to write their thoughts in Spanish as well.

As he began the lesson in his class he asked, "What do you imagine when you think of a Spanish speaker?" He immediately asked them to write down three ways to describe the person they imagined. As they finished writing their responses, he asked students to share some of their responses. He allowed students to openly share their responses for a few minutes before he moved on by asking them what they based their responses on. He asked if they were based on personal experience, television, movies, the Internet, and so on. As students responded, he brought up his PowerPoint on the projector for students to see. As their attention turned toward the PowerPoint, he began to explain what he would be sharing with them.

He asked the class to focus on the pictures he was going to show them and to share if they thought the individual was Latino or was not, and to guess the individual's profession. The pictures he showed them were not titled. The pictures were of Victor Cruz (professional football player), Saul "Canelo" Alverez (professional boxer), Carlos Slim (billionaire businessman), Alexis Bledel (actress), Sofia Vergara (actress), Cameron Diaz (actress), and Peter Gene Hernandez, better known as Bruno Mars (singer-songwriter). As they went through the pictures, students recognized some but ultimately struggled with determining who was Latino.

As they finished going through the PowerPoint, they discussed as a class the diversity among Latinos and the stereotypes associated with how people look. He further connected people being stereotyped to what students in class had shared in the past, and he gave them an opportunity to share what it felt like to be stereotyped. Students shared openly and felt connected to what he was teaching about Latinos and the Spanish language. As he moved on from what people looked like and the stereotypes associated with them, he introduced them to the topic of clothing. He asked them to share their thoughts on one aspect of "code switching," when people wear professional clothing versus casual clothing. As students began to discuss this, he divided students into groups and handed out magazines that were in Spanish for them to use. He asked students to pick clothing within the magazines and describe them, discuss the clothing together, and write summaries of their thoughts on the clothing—all in Spanish.

His students were engaged with this alternative lesson and found it relevant, as the connection was initially made through stereotypes and made the entire process interactive for students so they would take part. For a group of students who, at face value, did not seem interested in learning or participating in their Spanish class, this teacher was able to engage them, generate an interest, and teach them the material they needed to learn. Overall, his alternative lesson took 35 minutes in his class and was, according to the teacher, easy to create.

These three examples of alternative lessons highlight the diversity found among alternative lessons. They are unique to each teacher, yet they all share the same fundamental foundation.

Alternative lessons take very little time to create and can have a major impact on the learning process for students. Creating alternative lessons can also be fun, quite different from the dreadful feeling that accompanies the time and work teachers put into traditional lesson plans that may yield little, if any, return. As mentioned earlier, as educators, we sometimes become complacent with our own academic and personal growth. Alternative lessons help break through these barriers because they force us to grow continually on multiple levels. More important is their ability to help us expand our knowledge base: We simply learn more as we create alternative lessons for our students. This constant learning further benefits our students because as we grow, we can share what helps us grow with our students. That, in turn, helps them find ways to grow continually as well. Alternative lessons not only are fun to create but also take little time to generate. Implementing them maximizes positive outcomes in class because alternative lessons are the perfect complement to Real Talk, building and sustaining teachers' connectedness and success with their students over time.

# 11

## *Training and Feedback*

The final component in the training of teachers is the process of creating Real Talks and alternative lessons to implement in their classes. The rate at which teachers apply the approach varies. Teachers, instructors, and professors should try to keep a comfortable pace as they begin to apply the pedagogy in their classes. Keep in mind that I am suggesting a framework for training teachers, but ultimately it is up to the individual to determine how to best train others in this approach. In some cases, educators will want to ease into using the whole pedagogy or parts of it over the course of a semester or academic year, while others may be comfortable immediately implementing part or all of the approach.

Whenever possible, teachers should be given templates for Real Talks and alternative lessons. Assign teachers homework, asking them to outline or create three Real Talks and five alterative lessons to use during the first semester of their implementation of the Pedagogy of Real Talk. Then have the teachers form small groups to share and discuss their ideas with one another. This supports their creation of powerful, effective, and efficient Real Talks and alternative lessons. By focusing first on Real Talks and then on alternative lessons, teachers can begin the implementation process slowly rather than overwhelming themselves in their first attempts to apply these concepts in their classrooms. Teachers can also see how Real Talk and alternative lessons complement one another.

Regardless of when you begin creating Real Talks and alternative lessons, give teachers two weeks for each concept. Before they ever apply anything in class, go over what they have created and help those who are struggling to produce something they can use in their classes. This process is usually eye opening because the teachers will learn much about themselves and one another. The collaborative work in which the teachers engage also contributes to a positive and effective culture within their schools.

Teachers vary in their comfort and understanding in creating Real Talks. When you meet as a group, have teachers individually share what they have produced or where they are struggling. As you help them identify strengths and offer suggestions for strengthening their Real Talks, the teachers should also help one another, especially giving help to those who are struggling. For example, one math teacher completely understood the concept and applicability of Real Talk after her training and tried creating her own Real Talks (see Appendix D). She was one of the stronger teachers, adapting and incorporating the pedagogy quickly and effectively.

However, one of her colleagues, who was passionate, willing, and eager to apply Real Talks, struggled to create them. She was visibly frustrated with the process as everyone shared the Real Talks they had created. She struggled with how to keep Real Talks from turning into counseling sessions that consume the entire class hour (i.e., losing control) and with sharing components of herself within Real Talks.

As I worked with her, other teachers began to help her understand how to use Real Talk in the classroom. We first approached the teacher's struggle with sharing components of herself. This stemmed from her fear of students judging her or using what they learned against her in the classroom. Her colleagues helped her identify aspects of her life that were unique and interesting that she was comfortable sharing without revealing anything that was uncomfortable for her. Thus, with the help of her colleagues, she overcame this issue and began to create Real Talks (see Appendix E).

We also addressed her concern about losing control of the class. I shared with her and the other teachers that there always needs to be an ending to the Real Talk. How this occurs is up to the teacher and will vary from teacher to teacher. One thing to do is to set a specific time frame to know when to wrap up the discussion. Real Talk can range from five to 20 minutes or longer, depending on student involvement and teacher discretion. Teachers should also refer back to the work students must do in class, regardless of the type of Real Talk used. Once teachers understand and accept that they are the ones who determine when to use Real Talk, the type of Real Talk to use, and the length of time needed to accomplish the purpose of the Real Talk, they will remain in control of the discussion and guide it back to the work students must accomplish. In some cases, when students are sharing powerful things, the teacher must be tactful in pulling the class back to their work. This ensures students do not feel disregarded. Teachers may openly share that they are willing to talk with students further immediately after class or at a designated time, making sure to follow through on these promises. Following through with students is very important. Not doing so can potentially damage the relationship between teacher and student. Ultimately, however, learning when to end discussion and transition back to regular classwork is a matter of practice. It takes time to learn to recognize the best time to end Real Talks.

After the teachers solidify their Real Talks for the semester, I have them begin collecting information about their students' terministic screens through what they revealed during the Real Talks. How they accomplish this varies from teacher to teacher. In some cases, teachers write down what they learn about students' terministic screens as soon as their students leave the class. Some teachers wait until the end of the day to reflect and write down what they had learned about their students. Others simply remembered everything they had learned about their students without having to write anything down. Thus, teachers can accomplish this part of the training in whatever manner is easiest and most comfortable for them as long as they find a way to remember what they learn about their students' terministic screens.

As students reveal their terministic screens, teachers should immediately reevaluate their Real Talks to ensure they were appropriate. When necessary, they can use the information they learned to adjust the Real Talks to make them more appropriate for connecting with their students. Thus, teachers begin implementing the flexibility component of the pedagogy to ensure consistent success in working with their students at risk. To be receptive to their students' needs, at times, teachers only need to change the components of their Real Talks slightly. Other times, teachers may need to make significant changes, even to the point of creating an entirely different Real Talk. Sometimes teachers can make these changes outside class time; at other times, they can adapt their Real Talks as they are occurring in class. However, because of the emphasis on flexibility during the training, when changes are needed, the teachers adapt quite well. By the end of the third Real Talk of the semester, teachers will have a firm understanding of their students' terministic screens.

Teachers use what they have learned from their students to produce alternative lessons that resonate with their different terministic screens. Ideally try to give teachers two weeks to create five alternative lessons to use during the semester. As previously done, at the end of the two weeks, meet as a group to share lessons and to help each other strengthen everyone's alternative lessons. As with the development of the Real Talks, some teachers grasp the concept and begin developing lessons more quickly than others.

The decision to have teachers create and implement Real Talks first and then produce alternative lessons is strategic: Doing so focuses teachers on the most difficult yet powerful component of the pedagogy first. Because these two components are the most challenging to create, sustain, and implement successfully in the classroom, you want to make sure teachers are successful before moving forward to the other components of the approach. Even so, as it is appropriate to do so, introduce other elements of the pedagogy as the teachers learn to develop both the

Real Talks and the alternative lessons. Because teachers vary in their strengths and areas needing improvement, flexibility is the key to the pedagogy. It allows teachers to adapt as needed to incorporate the pedagogy into their classrooms. Thus, teachers customize the training to meet their needs in the classroom, adopting the pedagogy in its entirety or incorporating specific components to fill the gaps they have identified in their teaching repertoire.

Feedback from teachers and administrators alike has been overwhelmingly positive, as they have noted the changes in their classrooms. For example, disciplinary referrals have decreased in many cases. Because of the students' behavioral issues, many of the teachers shared concerns about being able to teach students successfully. As teachers began incorporating the Pedagogy of Real Talk, they noticed students exhibited fewer behavioral issues. Another major issue for teachers of students at risk is attendance. Before we can teach them, we must first get students to attend class. By implementing Real Talk and alternative lessons, teachers found that student attendance improved and became more consistent. Teachers and administrators also shared that the relationships they established through using Real Talk in their classrooms led to levels of connectedness with their students that they had never experienced in the past. They clearly experienced the reasons Real Talk is a key component in teaching students successfully. It enables teachers to establish genuine and powerful connections with their students, turning their classrooms into places students want to be.

Many teachers have been very surprised with how quickly they begin to see positive changes with their students and how easy it is to apply the approach. Because the implementation of the Pedagogy of Real Talk is designed to be flexible, it can be adapted to meet the needs of any teacher. It provides a framework teachers can use to build a solid pedagogical foundation by incorporating the different components of the pedagogy in a manner that allows every teacher to be authentic in the classrooms. All any teacher needs to incorporate this pedagogy is a wholehearted willingness to try it. Its design is such that teachers can implement it rather seamlessly into their existing programs.[1] One teacher who experienced newfound success in her classroom summarized it in this way:

> My principal wanted to come see me teach because my passing rates and relationship with students had become so overwhelming positive he wanted to see firsthand what I was doing. When he came to observe, I did a Real Talk and did what I learned through the pedagogy as I usually did. At the end of his visit, he

---

[1]See appendices for more examples of Real Talks and alternative lessons.

approached me and said that he was not sure what I was doing but he could see how engaged and eager the students were to learn from me.

Through the Pedagogy of Real Talk, teachers are not trying to become something they are not. Rather, among many things, they are learning to be true to themselves and to their students in a systematic manner that translates into success in the classroom.

# 12

## *New Beginnings*

For far too long, our schools have been plagued with a dropout epidemic. We cannot afford to let millions of students drop out of school each year. We cannot simply give up on students at risk or blame them for the circumstances that have contributed to their rejection of traditional school cultures. As professionals, we are responsible for finding ways to reach every student entrusted to our care, not just the ones who are easy to teach or who learn what we set before them easily. Our challenge is to reach the seemingly unreachable. But no student is completely unreachable. It just takes one teacher willing to go beyond the usual parameters of traditional pedagogy to make the difference in a student's life. We must remember that it is the students who need us the most who will push us away the most.

I spent my entire K–12 experience identified as a student at risk. When I found a teacher that I felt truly connected with, I performed well in class. I had the ability, but my life circumstances, my rejection of school norms, my not seeing anything relevant in what was being taught, and my lack of meaningful connections with teachers caused me to feel that school was a place for everyone except me. I felt like an impostor sitting in my classes, that my rightful place was in the streets. Teachers did not understand the hatred I had for school. Adding to my isolation, I'd been taught to show no signs of weakness and not to ask questions. I was not unique in this sense; a population of students who shared my sentiments and were at risk of dropping out of school existed decades before me, and they will exist decades after me. These experiences, however, were the foundation for creating something not only fundamentally sound but also infused with passion that can increase passing rates for students at risk. Rather than highlighting the timeless epidemic of students at risk dropping out of school and feeling overwhelmed by it, I chose to create a timeless approach to help reduce this epidemic.

Simply teaching students and having them learn may work for teachers of the college-bound students. These students adapt to teachers, curriculum, subjects, rules, and lessons because they accept that they must do these things to go to college. Students at risk do not adjust in this manner, which results in an adversarial relationship with teachers and schools. Overcoming this kind of relationship becomes very difficult when teachers receive more and more students at risk into their classroom, many of whom have made up their minds not to like their teachers before even meeting them.

After working with thousands of educators, I have come to realize how very isolating teaching in the classroom can be. Many of us know this, but we seldom discuss it. Although we work in institutions alongside colleagues, once we enter the arena of our classrooms, we face the overwhelming task of teaching a large group of students on a day-to-day basis. The pressure is immense. As days turn into months, the isolation we feel as educators in the American education system solidifies. Given the rigors of teaching, we can easily become complacent. But it is crucial for us to resist. Complacency will only hurt both the students and us, the teachers, in the classroom.

Breaking through the constraints of complacency is complicated by the highly personal nature of pedagogy. Teaching is a personal craft, an art form. Because it is so personal, some people have difficulty accepting that they need to improve or possibly completely revamp what they do in their classrooms. We must accept that as human beings, we will always have opportunities to grow and improve. Being educators is no different. The most successful educators I have met were willing to accept their need for growth in certain areas and searched for ways to improve their teaching continually to increase the performance and passing rates of their most challenging students.

Any educator willing to build connections with students and to adapt to meet the needs of their students can use the Pedagogy of Real Talk in any subject area. Educators of any student-at-risk population can implement the Pedagogy of Real Talk to help their students succeed. At the core of the pedagogy is the breaking down of socially constructed barriers and the establishing of meaningful connections between educators and students. Creating honest and open communication between educators and their students, giving students a voice in shaping their classroom environments, and allowing students to teach their teachers as they are taught by their teachers empower students to learn. However, the ability to relate to students is a skill that is not easily taught. Only through actual face-to-face interactions with students can educators establish such relatedness.

Educators must also be willing to stray from their comfort zone and take a genuine interest in their students' lives while sharing components of their own lives to begin to build relationships with students. Understanding that students are people before they are students is essential in establishing meaningful connections. Making connections with students is not a one-dimensional approach in which students share and educators merely listen. Rather, it is a process whereby students can comfortably feel and say that they know who their teacher is as a person, thus establishing and recognizing effective relationships. As educators begin sincerely and effectively to relate to their students at risk, they will create opportunities to learn about their students' terministic screens. By using students' terministic screens to create dynamic lessons that maximize student engagement, educators can build the connections needed to reach their students. Integral to this process are the Real Talk discussions.

Real Talk is very powerful and can be used on its own or in unison with the pedagogy in its entirety to maximize its effectiveness. However, mastering Real Talk is a process. Educators must be both patient and willing to learn how to use it effectively in their classrooms. Although Real Talk is one of the most challenging pieces in the pedagogy, over the years, I have witnessed educators who have learned to use it appropriately to transform not only the lives of their students but their own lives as well. Many of the educators I worked with truly had a passion to help their students. However, they simply were not finding the tools they needed to realize their passion. Real Talk is a tool educators can use to achieve success in a manner many educators no longer believe is possible. Many of these educators feel it is impossible to establish meaningful connections with their students that will result in improving the performance of their students at risk. Thus, with Real Talk, educators revitalize themselves and their careers.

Establishing success from semester to semester is something that only strengthens the approach. Educators achieve this continual success by adapting the pedagogy to meet the needs of their students and their classes. Adaptability is not a unique characteristic of this teaching style. It is a skill that any willing educator with a drive to engage students can incorporate. Many students at risk around the country have difficulty seeing the relevancy, importance, or connection of the material educators want them to learn. Their lack of connection with their teachers also stands in their way of learning. Educators accept education as a long-term investment for success and may not fathom the idea of rejecting school. Students at risk, however, are more entrenched in their present and the difficulties they face in their daily lives. They may have difficulty imagining or understanding how their education will affect the next 20 years of their lives. By being adaptable, educators will understand their students better, enabling them to find avenues through which they can help students adopt education as a form of empowerment within their lives. In fact, when instructors are willing, the students themselves will often express their need for adaptation and will contribute ideas for restructuring lessons to make them more effective.

It's not a common practice for teachers to consistently engage students at risk in the learning process. For many students, learning school material is a tedious process. This tedium is even more pronounced for students who reject school norms, as many students at risk do. The Pedagogy of Real Talk allows educators to repair the damage done to so many of these students. Through this pedagogy, we can let our students know who we are and that we care about them, about who they are, and about what they need to survive and to rise above their circumstances. We can prepare them to overcome any future inequality they may encounter. We can teach them not only to be successful in our classes but also to embrace education, preparing them for the academic challenges they will face in the future. Helping students at risk transform from rejecting school to embracing it is a monumental accomplishment for any educator. It is a humbling experience to witness students willing to learn and having fun in the classroom without feeling disdain towards learning.

Dread, intimidation, and feelings of hopelessness do not have to exist for educators who work with students at risk. Throughout my years of teaching, working with educators, and in having been a student at risk, I have witnessed countless passionate educators become jaded, almost cynical, as the daily grind of teaching disengaged students wore them down. To see the light of passion in teachers' eyes again and to bring that passion to the forefront of their teaching is transforming not only for the teachers but also for their students. The disadvantaged backgrounds of some students at risk do not have to result in their academic disadvantage in the classroom. By developing inclusive, structured, student-oriented learning environments and incorporating methods and strategies to build better connections with students, educators can reach students at risk and help them achieve academically. We can help them become successful, fulfilled, productive members of society. The Pedagogy of Real Talk is designed to do just that. I encourage all educators to begin implementing The Pedagogy of Real Talk in classrooms today. Start small, but start. Break down the barriers that prevent educators and students from reaching high levels of success together.

Time is too precious to wait for the next semester or the next school year. Too many passionate, highly skilled teachers are drowning in classes where they are trying so desperately to help their students succeed. Teachers are feeling pressure from administrators and city, state, and federal governments to stop the elevated dropout rates. Rather than sit and argue about who is to blame for these dropout rates, teachers must be the first to take action, to lead by example as we slowly but surely garner the support of the education system. We must be willing to incorporate viable approaches to bolster our success in the classroom.

The Pedagogy of Real Talk can be that approach. Educators who are already practicing some components of the approach can adopt the remaining components to fill the gaps in their pedagogical repertoire. Educators currently using approaches that are quite different from the Pedagogy of Real Talk can choose to adopt this new pedagogy instead, completely revamping their teaching approach. Time is of the essence. Students at risk don't have time to waste, and we cannot allow students to continue to drop out of school.

As I reflect on the creation and implementation of the Pedagogy of Real Talk, I can't help but smile as I see the faces of the numerous students I have had the privilege of serving directly or indirectly through the educators who are using the approach. I am always filled with excitement as I walk into classrooms filled with students at risk. They remind me that coming up with a pedagogical game plan is easy for individuals far away from the classroom; it is another thing entirely to be the person in the classroom who has to implement the approach with a group of uninterested students. Every educator has a game plan before walking into the classroom, but it only takes a few minutes with a group of students at risk before the educator is tossing that plan out the window. The Pedagogy of Real Talk was not created in a room or an office far removed from the classrooms of students at risk. It took form thanks to the teachers and students who informed and sharpened its uniqueness, applicability, and success. The Pedagogy of Real Talk is a solid fundamental base yet is purposely flexible to allow educators to adapt to the uniqueness of every person willing to use it with their students. Any pedagogy created without taking the uniqueness of each individual and the differences between people into account will be too rigid to be successful with all students. The Pedagogy of Real Talk is a flexible tool that will work for all types, styles, and personalities of educators who are sincerely willing to try it and who strive to grow.

My hope is that educators, students, school districts, and society will all benefit from the success we can establish in the classroom for a population of students for whom success has been elusive for many generations. I am hopeful that based on what I have provided, people not only will find the pedagogy useful and sustainable over time but also will improve on it whenever possible. Pedagogy is a constantly evolving process that must continually grow within the minds of the individuals who practice it in their classrooms. This constant growth will only further contribute to the success of those we ultimately serve in our classrooms, our students. If I am fortunate, I will live to see this work further enhanced by the brilliant minds that exist in our world, perhaps those of other students at risk who not only beat the odds stacked against them but also set a new standard for how we view and value intellect within our society.

# *Appendices*

This section contains diverse examples from my own collection and from those of teachers who have successfully used the pedagogy with varying student populations (e.g., rural, urban, diverse racial groups, homogeneous racial groups, varying social classes). I share these samples to give teachers a better understanding of how to apply Real Talks and alternative lessons in the classroom and to show the diversity and creativity possible within these components. In Appendices F, G, and H, teachers will find sample Real Talks. In Appendix I, teachers will find a few themes and Real Talk summaries about how I used Real Talks with my students. Appendices J, K, L, M, and N are alternative lessons. Appendix O contains titles and summaries of alternative lessons I used in my classes.

It is important to remember that the alternative lessons shared here were very successful in part because students had first participated in Real Talks. The lessons were introduced after teachers achieved their intended goals for the Real Talks.

Educators should also understand that the effective and consistent use of Real Talks and alternative lessons can sometimes lead to quite unexpected positive results. Within my classes, students began creating educational games to play in class (Appendix P). Not only were these games very creative and fun to play, but they also maintained the focus of learning on the material the students needed to pass the GED. Students who admittedly had never participated in class before, especially in classroom games, became involved and learned. This was, in my mind, an added bonus and testament to the success of the Pedagogy of Real Talk.

In providing these examples, I hope educators will use them as a springboard in applying the Pedagogy of Real Talk within their classrooms. I hope they will serve as templates teachers can use to build their own diverse repertoire of instructional strategies. Most of all, I hope teachers will see how others have worked within the components of the Pedagogy of Real Talk to build classrooms in which both students at risk and teachers are successful.

As you read through the Real Talks, keep in mind that they may look different than the suggested format discussed in Chapter 9. As mentioned there, everyone's Real Talk will look different as the delivery is meant to be customized by the person delivering the Real Talk.

# *Appendix A*

## *Real Talk on Symbolism*

**I** had to create a Real Talk to introduce students to symbolism because it was a section of the reading component of the GED exam. This Real Talk was for a different class and group of students than those discussed in Chapter 9 regarding adversity. I created it because the students were neither receptive to discussing symbolism nor aware of its importance. They wanted to skip this section, which many of them referred to as "stupid" or "boring." Because the students were struggling to understand symbolism based on their previous experiences, I also sensed an element of fear. Therefore, I created a Real Talk that began by focusing on our lives and eventually connected to the symbolism section in the GED.

| | |
|---|---|
| **Teacher:** | Let me ask you all something very specific today. How has being away from home been since you have been here at MSU? I mean, specifically, how has it made you miss or maybe not miss home? For example, what does "home" mean to you now that you have experienced living at MSU? |
| **Student A:** | That's a good question; and to be honest, I have thought about it a lot. For me, home means family. That's where my heart is. I mean, I get it that home is all fucked up cause it's the ghetto; but it is still home for me and I love it. |
| **Teacher:** | Okay, so are you saying that home means family to you? |
| **Student A:** | Yes. |
| **Teacher:** | Anyone else willing to share their thoughts on this? |
| **Student B:** | I never thought of home in the past because I was |

there every day and had never left. Now that I finally left, I see things differently. All of the stuff that happens back home has been negative for me. So for me, home means a place I don't want to go back to; and if I can, I want to stay here at MSU.

Teacher:    So tell us in one word or a few what home means to you.

Student B:    It means drama that I don't need or want.

Teacher:    Okay, so home in this case means drama. One more person want to share?

Student C:    Home for me is where all of my experiences have happened. Like good ones and bad ones. So coming here, I know I am willing to leave home for a while so I can get my education; but I want to go back.

Teacher:    Why do you want to go back?

Student C:    'Cause to me home is my heart. It's what made me the way I am today; and I ain't fucking perfect, but I'm a good person who has been through a lot of stuff. I know people judge us when we come from the hood in all kinds of negative ways; but for real, I'm not ashamed of where I am from.

Teacher:    So home represents your heart?

Student C:    Yes.

Teacher:    Okay, as you can all see and have already thought about for yourselves, home means something very powerful for all of us, sometimes in similar ways and very different other times. Like for me, home was the only place I knew growing up, and I just accepted what it was. But when I went away and started seeing and experiencing new things, I would think back to home; and I would become really angry. I would think back to home and I was angry at all the deep poverty and inequality that I went through and that exists where I came from. So home was a painful memory. But, eventually, I got to a place where home was where my heart will always be; and I embraced and appreciated everything I learned, both good and bad, because it allowed me to become who I am today. It gave me strength and insight that I would not have gotten anywhere else, and now home is a place that gives me strength wherever I am in the world. I ain't trippin' that I no longer live back home because home exists in my heart; and it symbolizes my strength when I feel weak. Does this make sense to everyone?

**Various Students**: Yes.

Yeah, I feel you.

Yup.

**Teacher**: Okay, what we just did was use symbolism within our own lives. You see, we all have something that reminds us of something else—whether it is home and what it symbolizes to us or when you think of what America symbolizes to each of you, what police departments symbolize for us, or how when you think of a certain type of animal it may represent power or agility or speed, etc., to us. The point is that symbolism is a part of our everyday lives, and we all use it in similar and, at times, very different ways. We have to use what you just did with me in a way now that focuses these same ideas on figuring out how the GED uses symbolism in some of the questions you will be asked on the exam. So I need your help in being open to trying to learn about symbolism from the standpoint of what you are going to be learning from your books today. So, you all ready to get cracking on the symbolism section?

**Various Students**: Yeah, let's do it.

I'm with it.

A'ight.

# *Appendix B*

## *"Who I Am" Real Talk on the First Day of Class*

This is the Real Talk I used with my students on the first day of class. It is an excellent way to show students that you are a real person, not an adversary, that your position as teacher is only one facet of who you are. Using this Real Talk will help you set the tone for the way you will conduct class.

**Teacher**:   Good morning, class. My name is Dr. Paul Hernandez and I want not only to welcome you but, if you give me the chance, to share a little bit about myself and how and why I teach in the manner I do. Let me show you who I am as a person before you decide that I am simply a teacher.

[Students are staring at me with looks of bewilderment, curiosity, and, in some cases, defensiveness.]

Standing in front of you is a former dropout and someone who not only struggled in school but hated everything about it. I remember many different occasions when I was told that I was dumb or that I was better off just going to work instead of being in school. I was treated more like a "thing" rather than a person. It was a punishment for me to have to go to school; but ultimately, it was not because I was stupid or because I was lazy. There were many other things going on in my life that affected my ability to put school as number one in my life. Combining my life with being treated disrespectfully by some educators, it pushed me to eventually walk away from school.

[Students perk up and listen more intently as they focus on what I am sharing.]

It was all of the harsh challenges I faced from growing up in deep poverty with my momma, who was a single mother; the road blocks that were put in front of me by haters who wanted to see me fail; or the fact that I was raised within the gang culture of Los Angeles—all played a role in why I stand in front of you here today.

[Students are captivated by what is being said. They say nothing, but their attention is directed at me. You can hear a pin drop in the class. A few are still showing resistance with their body language but are focusing on what I am saying.]

This class and what I have to offer is all about you and finding a way to have you pass the sections of the GED we are preparing to take. But we will not just focus on our book; we will incorporate the real world and our experiences into this class.

For me, it's an honor to have the opportunity to work with you; and with your help, I know we can turn this class into something positive and different than any other class you have ever had. If you give me the opportunity, not only will we learn how to pass the GED; but we will also grow in order to get ready to succeed beyond the GED.

You will get to know me and I will get to know you; but I want you to see the real me, and I hope you let me see the real you as it will help us in making sure we work well together as we move forward. For me, it was my education that ultimately helped me reach heights that I never imagined; and even as I stand here in front of you, I can't even believe I made it out of the situations I faced throughout my life. Now, do you have any questions before we get started with the work we have to start chipping away at?

**Various Students**:    Damn, that's some real shit.

Did you ever meet your dad?

I already like this class.

I ain't ever had a teacher talk to me the way you just did.

How old are you?

Is your mom proud of you?

# *Appendix C*

## *Real Talk on Adversity*

The teacher is in front of the room as students enter the class. Informal conversation takes place between the students and teacher as students settle in and prepare for the class.

**Teacher**: Class, may I have your attention? How is everyone doing today? How are you doing today, Jay? How was last night? You feeling all right?

**Student A**: I'm all right. I'm feeling a little tired because I didn't sleep much last night. But it's all good because I was studying and I am ready for Round 2 today.

**Teacher**: Good! I'm glad you are studying! If you have any specific questions, just holler at me. But try to find a balance because I want you to feel rested because I want you to keep learning. This goes for all of you. Work hard but find a balance so you feel rested and ready to work every day.

[Students are starting to listen intently; a few students are raising their hands to respond to the initial question.]

**Teacher**: Big T, what do you wanna share?

**Student B**: It's hard to find a balance. Sometimes I wanna work all night and sometimes I don't wanna do shit.

**Teacher**: That's a great point. I feel like that sometimes myself. Does anyone else feel like it's difficult to find a balance sometimes?

**Various Students:**    Yeah.

Shit's hard.

It's a struggle.

For sure.

Yeah, sometimes life ain't easy.

**Teacher:**    You see, the thing we are talking about right now is dealing with adversity. Adversity means hard times, and we all go through hard times in this world. Regardless of where we come from, everyone struggles in their own way at some point in their lives to make it through a day, a week, a month, a year.

For me, adversity has meant so many different things. Adversity when I was a kid meant having a single mother who worked as hard as she could yet we had nothing. My momma was forced to work seven days a week and 15 hours day; so as much as she tried to be there for us, she struggled to find a balance. I remember as a little boy the daily struggles were not knowing if we would have anything to eat, a place to live, and if we would even survive to see the next day. Even though I had my brothers and my momma, I felt isolated and alone, living in a world that did not care if I would live or die. That was the type of adversity I dealt with as a kid, and I always felt that no one understood what I was going through.

When I went to community college, adversity meant something else. I had to learn and teach myself how to pay attention, take notes, and even care about passing a class. Just trying to focus, forcing myself to go to class after a whole 12-hour shift of work was a struggle. I mean, it was so much easier to just give up, throw in the towel, walk away, and put in overtime to make a few extra bucks. Trying to go to school, succeed in school, and make a dream come true was a daily challenge. I had no one to help me but myself. You feel me? You understand what I am telling you?

**Various Students:**    Yeah, I feel you.

You are right; it's a struggle.

I can't believe you had to go through that.

Yeah, man, it has been tough.

**Teacher:**    You see, I could tell you stories about my struggles all day, but the point of this is to figure out what struggles you go through so we can figure out how to beat them and succeed in the class. This ain't about me; it's about you. What's standing in your way to make this GED come true? What stood in your way in the past that makes you think or worry that you can't make it to college? 'Cause I am here to tell you that we are going to make this thing happen.

Student C:    It's always been hard having so many people in the family and everyone being broke. It's hard to focus 'cause you just wanna help your family. You wanna go work and bring money home to make sure everyone can eat. This is the type of thing that was always riding my mind when I tried the school thing. I ain't gonna lie; I think about this all the time. That's why it's so hard being here.

Teacher:    Trust me when I say we all feel you. You are not the only one in this room who feels an obligation to his family. But what you just shared is the type of thing I need you all to be open about so we can figure out what doesn't allow us to focus on the work at hand.

Student D:    Yeah, it's hard 'cause I think of my kids. And I want to be there and support them, but I know I gotta be here to get my GED.

Student E:    I'm worried that I'm out here trying this shit, and all my people are proud of me but I'm not gonna make it. I ain't scared of shit, but I don't wanna let everybody down.

Teacher:    That's it! You see, every single one of us in here has these daily challenges. Our biggest challenge sitting here in this class is preparing to pass this GED. Everything you guys have talked about we can improve by improving ourselves by passing and getting the GED. Getting the GED will be the manner in which we overcome adversity this semester. Getting the GED will open up new doors for us. These new doors will allow you to better yourself with jobs, more schooling that can help with your families back home. As a class, in my class, together we will overcome the adversity we face in the GED. Now, you feeling me? You see me? This is the kind of thing I wanna discuss in class in order to keep us motivated and focused on passing the GED. It will not be easy at times, but we will overcome the adversity we face with preparing to pass the GED together.

What we are going to do now is take these thoughts on adversity, these things you shared with me, and write them down. We must practice the fundamental writing techniques that will support your GED writing as we discussed yesterday in Lesson 8 and Lesson 10 regarding a strong topic sentence in your essay, clear transition sentences, and phrases. So let's turn to these sections in your books and get ready to get some work done.

# *Appendix D*

## *Real Talk on Assumptions*

This is a summary of a Real Talk used by a teacher who I trained in the Pedagogy of Real Talk. As with other teachers I have worked with, I asked her to use a template to record her use of Real Talk in the classroom.

This teacher teaches math. The specific unit in her geometry class for this Real Talk was congruent triangles. Based on her experiences in teaching that class, students were not interested in this topic. Students shutting down before ever beginning any work or hearing any lecture on congruent triangles made teaching this unit very difficult for the teacher. She wanted to create a Real Talk to generate interest, make the topic less threatening, establish receptiveness on the part of the students, and make the material relevant to them. The teacher did this by creating a Real Talk focused on assumptions and used it as a warm-up activity.

She posed these questions to her students: "What are some pros and cons of making assumptions? Have people ever made assumptions about you? How did that make you feel? Why do people make assumptions?" She had them first write out their responses. Then she had them share their responses as a class. She began the Real Talk by sharing how people make assumptions about her because she teaches at an alternative education school. This was something that students related to strongly because they attended the alternative education school. She then became more specific as she moved down the Real Talk funnel, sharing that teachers had sometimes made negative assumptions of her when she was in school. Based on the way she dressed and the friends she had, teachers had assumed she was a bad student; so they were surprised that she was a good student.

After she shared her personal component, she asked her students if they had anything to share about making assumptions. The teacher stated that although not all of her students spoke up, the entire class was visibly engaged. Those who did speak up shared many powerful and relevant things about the theme. Many shared how they dealt with negative assumptions about them because they were alternative education students or because they had certain life circumstances. Those circumstances led many of them to share how they were victims of negative assumptions. Students shared what it was like to be a single mother. They shared racial issues and social class issues that they tied into the assumptions made about them.

Beyond the verbal participation of the students, she noted other things that were not common with her students. Many students wrote a great deal regarding her Real Talk, yet writing was something her students did not cooperate with her in doing. Her Real Talk, however, spurred the students to write long responses to the questions she had posed. She also had her students work in small groups after the Real Talk. She seldom did this because her students typically refused to work with others, especially with students who were not their friends. In this case, her students were willing not only to work in groups but also to work in groups where some students were not their friends—and they worked well together on the work assigned for that day.

Ultimately, she ended the Real Talk by introducing the connection between making assumptions and the unit on congruent triangles. She explained to the class that "the idea of assumptions tied into the unit's curriculum, as we were going to make assumptions about triangles, and we needed to be careful that we had enough information to prove our assumptions were correct."

The teacher's reflections on the Real Talk were that it had an overwhelmingly positive effect on her students. She had generated interest, made the topic less threatening, established student receptiveness, and made it relevant to them. She knew she had made a lasting impression when later in the semester she shared that she had a positive experience with a few of her students based on her Real Talk: "Later on in the semester, a few students made comments back to the Real Talk (e.g., 'You can't make assumptions, Ms. X!'), so it seems to have stuck with them." Finally, the teacher shared that she had enjoyed conducting the Real Talk and had personally seen the difference it had made in her class.

# *Appendix E*

## *Real Talk on Overcoming Personal Challenges With Hard Work and Determination*

This is a very good example of a Real Talk because it shows how teachers can vary how to start or generate Real Talks in their classes yet include the content described in the definition of Real Talk. This one also shows how students can unknowingly help determine the topic to be discussed in class when they openly share something. Through their formal training, teachers can recognize and use what students share in class in an authentic, empathetic, and systematic manner.

The teacher who conducted this Real Talk teaches English and social studies. In the first week of school, she had her students fill out a questionnaire about their personal and educational backgrounds. After the students completed the survey, she asked the class if they would be willing to share anything about themselves. The class was quiet for a few minutes until a female student spoke up. She shared that she was often called a slut because she had a two-year-old son. Being called that made her feel like a loser who would not be successful in life. Then a male student spoke up and shared that he also had a son. He elaborated that he struggled with being a responsible parent and a good role model for his child, especially because he was nearly a high school dropout.

The teacher seized the opportunity to connect the universal theme of personal challenges to the class by sharing her own experience growing up. Her parents were teenaged parents when she was born. They had faced monumental challenges as teenaged parents but slowly had succeeded by working very hard and sacrificing many things. They had eventually attended and graduated from college while raising their young family. She encouraged her students to feel free to ask questions if they had any. To her surprise, she was asked many questions, which she answered openly and honestly.

She kept the Real Talk with students flowing to help her students explicitly see the connection between hard work and determination in overcoming personal challenges. She concluded her Real Talk by sharing with her students that her parents had been married for 50 years because of their hard work, determination, and refusal to let people tell them they could not be successful.

This teacher felt the Real Talk had gone very well in her class. Her students were captivated throughout the entire process, and she felt a connection with her students. She explained that her students were positive and genuine in their interactions with her, which was not always a norm with students in her school. The teacher also shared that the next day she was approached by the female student who was a teenage mother. The girl told the teacher she had been surprised by what the teacher had shared with the class but thanked her for doing so. The girl continued that she now thought she could really be successful in life and eventually go to college.

# *Appendix F*

## *Real Talk on Transforming Frustration and Anger Into Empowerment*

**B**efore delving into this Real Talk, I must give some background about why this Real Talk was needed in my class. My students had recently been victims of racism at the university. The perpetrators in this case were a group of young college-aged men. As my students were walking across campus, they noticed a car full of young men that had driven by them multiple times. As my students were preparing for the worst, the young men in the car stuck their heads out and began yelling, "Go home, Mexicans!" "Go back to Mexico, fucking illegals!" "We don't want you in our country!" This encounter weighed heavily on them and threatened their ability to stay focused and to succeed because it had insinuated itself into the classroom. I gave this Real Talk to help my students stay in control and not throw away everything they had worked so hard for in class and the HEP program because of this negative experience. I had to reengage them, harness what they were feeling, and use it in a productive manner in the classroom. This Real Talk worked very well overall in helping them not lose control.

| | |
|---|---|
| **Teacher:** | What's going on with all of you? I can tell something is bothering you all. So what's up? |
| **Various Students:** | We were racially attacked yesterday! |
| | Fucking racists at this school! |
| | Fuck this place! |
| | I don't want to be here anymore 'cause I'm going to hurt someone! |
| **Teacher:** | Wow! Hold up! What happened? |

| **Student A:** | A bunch of White guys yelled from their car a bunch of racist shit to us and just took off as we started chasing down their car! That is some bullshit, and it's obvious people don't want us here! |
| --- | --- |
| **Teacher:** | Damn! I'm not going to make any excuses for what happened to you guys, but I don't want this to be a reason that it takes us away from all of the progress we have made with getting ready for the GED exam. |
| **Student B:** | Why should we do anything if this is what is always going to be in our lives? I am so mad! |
| **Teacher:** | Why? Because it is exactly what people who are against you would want you to do! Do you think the frustration and anger you feel over this is something new to this country or world? Hearing you all share this with me breaks my heart and reminds me of the racism I dealt with and deal with throughout my life. I know exactly how it feels, but I took time to understand how not to let it beat me. |
| **Student C:** | You dealt with racism before? |
| **Teacher:** | Hear me out for a second. I remember a time in my life that I was trying to decide if I was going to continue on with school or get further involved with things from the streets. Back then I would never have said this, but today I will gladly tell you: I was lost and hurt. The last thing I needed at that time was something else that was going to put me down or hurt me further. |
| **Various Students:** | What happened? |
| **Teacher:** | I was heading home on the bus from pretty far out from where I lived. I remember sitting towards the front of the bus. The area I was coming home from had very little diversity and the bus showed it. It was pretty full towards the back of the bus, but there were many empty seats around me. I remember this woman who got on the bus after I had been riding in the bus for a while. I remember when she got on to the bus I noticed how uniquely beautiful she was. So for just a few seconds, I admired her beauty; and as I was going to look away, she caught me glancing at her. As she looked at me while walking past me, I ignored her as I was slightly embarrassed; but what happened next I never expected. She sat next to |

another woman behind me. She then said, loud enough for me to hear, "Gross! Can you believe that Mexican was staring at me?" That was the last thing I needed to hear at that particular time in my life.

**Various Students:** Damn!

She is a bitch!

Damn, that ain't right!

What did you do?

**Teacher:** I stayed quiet and could hear her words echo in my mind as I stared out the window. I remember that at the moment I stared out and thought of what she said, I caught my reflection on the bus's windows and I could clearly see myself. I remember how I felt as I looked at myself. I was disgusted with myself and immediately was filled with anger and frustration. I wanted to take what I felt and hurt everyone around me. For me, at that time of my life, I ended up taking out that frustration on many others; and it only made things worse for me. It was the manner in which I responded that made things worse. The mistakes I made by responding the way I did is what I am hopeful you will not make today. You see, the things I know today I did not know back then; and I want to share them with you so you walk away stronger, better, and more successful than I did. I thought at the time that violence and revenge towards others was the answer, but I was wrong.

**Student D:** But I want to get them back for what they did to us!

**Teacher:** I know exactly what you mean, but we can get them back in a different way than what you have in mind. They want you to quit! They want you to walk away and not be a part of their world. But we will not do that. We will use what they have attacked you with as a source of strength to keep moving up and not only be a part of the world they want to exclude you from but you will become leaders in that world. The frustration and anger you feel should turn into motivation towards education. Your success will be payback to those who tried holding you down. You will be able to help get rid of the racism you felt by educating ignorant people regarding their stereotypes toward certain groups. Education will help give you the power to make sure that what you experienced yesterday will not happen to anyone else. If you quit on me now, then they have won and their attacks on you were successful. This is a perfect opportunity to use what you are feeling in a positive way in the classroom. Let's work together and take what we are feeling in order to beat the crap out of the GED exam!

**Various Students:**    Damn, Paul, you really know how to get us going again.

You're right. We can't let them win.

Yeah, I am still mad as hell; but if we do something stupid, we are going down and those racist assholes will still be out there doing their dirty shit. We just have to calm down and keep handling our business with this GED.

**Teacher:**    Okay, I know you are going to still feel upset and want to blow up when it gets bad, but we need to keep it together in class and when you are out of class stay cool. Because, remember, that things you do outside of class can affect you in class by getting in the way of what we have to do. I know what you are feeling, so let's take our time here to get back on track and you will see how it will pay off at the end.

# *Appendix G*

## *Real Talk on Being Authentic*

This particular Real Talk was created by an art teacher who had been teaching for over 25 years and initially struggled to grasp Real Talk. Her passion toward seeing her students succeed drove her to work hard to empower them. She was willing to learn something new and eventually created a Real Talk to try in her art lab. In this class, a majority of her students typically displayed feelings of trepidation. It was a challenge to get her students to let their defenses down to do art. She decided a Real Talk might be effective in doing so.

She began her Real Talk by sharing with her class an experience from college that had left an unforgettable impact on her as an artist and as a woman. Mr. M was one of her instructors who taught her about being authentic as a young college art student. Mr. M was terminally ill with cancer. His wife had also passed away, and he was raising his young children. In addition to all this, he was a paraplegic. She described him to the class as a man who had to use his upper body strength to propel his entire body, using crutches and dragging his legs to walk.

After describing the man, she explained that his doctors had strongly encouraged him to take numbing drugs (tranquilizers) to ease his physical and emotional pain. Mr. M had refused to do so because as an artist, he wanted to feel all of the emotions he carried. This teacher had felt bad for him because she could see how he loved so deeply. The love that Mr. M had for his wife had allowed him to feel both the positive emotions of having been with her and the painful emotions of having lost her. Mr. M had said that as an artist, he would not deny himself the experience of any of his emotions, especially the painful ones, explaining that without feeling the pain, he could never illustrate it in his art. To her, Mr. M was larger than life, one of the most authentic people she had ever met.

She continued that throughout her life the experience and message Mr. M conveyed gave her courage—the courage and inspiration to be authentic. She shared some brief experiences about being authentic: homeschooling her children, home birthing, and traveling around the world. These personal experiences were resources for her art and writing. She elaborated that, like a ripple in a pond, Mr. M continued to be her teacher. She then explained that she had allowed her students a peek into her journey as an artist so they could see that an artist must be willing to be courageous and authentic for their art to be successful. Lastly, she explained that in her art class, students should try to be in touch with themselves and reality. In this way, their artwork would be explosive, powerful, and compelling. She concluded her Real Talk by sharing that authenticity meant accepting yourself, knowing yourself, and having the courage to illustrate your truth.

The teacher told us that throughout the entire Real Talk, including a few seconds after she was done, the classroom was enveloped in a profound silence because the students were very quiet and listening intently. This type of attention was not a norm in her class. After the silence, students began to ask her questions about Mr. M, and several students began to share their own experiences. One young woman in her class shared how her uncle was as an inspiration to her because he battled and eventually overcame his addiction. The teacher was surprised that several students said goodbye to her after class and told her to have a nice day. This type of gesture was also not customary of her students. Another outcome of the Real Talk was that a young male student came to see the teacher during lunch to share with her his own personal story. The final outcome, she noted, occurred the next day in class: All her students greeted her, and they began to work with their art directly. This went on for several days, again not the type of behavior that was common for her students in the art lab.

# *Appendix H*

## *Real Talk on Classroom Norms*

This English teacher decided to use her first Real Talk on the first day of her class. After a training session, this teacher spoke to me about an idea for a Real Talk on drug use. She was nervous and not sure how to approach this issue. She had a great idea but needed a boost in her confidence and reassurance; she also needed someone to help her get the details straight for her delivery. Together, we solidified the approach for Real Talk.

On the first day of class, this teacher announced her classroom rules, specifically highlighting one rule that upset her students: Laying their heads down or sleeping/nodding off was not permitted in her class. She detailed that any student doing so would get a written referral. As always, when she shared this information with her students, they responded with resistance, complaining and speaking under their breath. The difference this time was that she had created a Real Talk to use at this point in the class.

She began by sharing with them an experience she had had in one of her classrooms that led to her creating this rule. Students were curious and began to listen as they realized that the rationale was directly connected to her experience with other students. A few years ago, the police had brought police dogs to search the school for drugs. She elaborately explained how chaotic everything was as the dogs searched and eventually found the drugs in her classroom. As she stood there listening to the dog barking excessively, she knew it had done its job. Her students at that time had sat calmly while the dog barked directly at one student. This experience had really shaken her up.

She then told her current students that her job was to help them succeed in school and to achieve their educational goals for the betterment of their lives. She couldn't compete with drugs in the classroom. She explained that teaching was not a backup job for her; it was her chosen career. She had gone to school for six years and had invested large amounts of her personal money to further her education to serve her students better. Her goal was ultimately to see her students graduate from high school and succeed with their lives. She could not reach those goals when her students chose drugs over school.

Rather than end the Real Talk, she moved to the next component, sharing another experience in her classroom that had happened within a few years. She had had a student who seemed to be sleepy or drowsy one afternoon and put his head down to sleep. She had told the student several times not to do so and had finally removed the student from class. When the student was taken to the administrator's office, the truth had been discovered: He had been having a very negative effect from the heroin he had taken earlier that day. Her removing him from class had helped ensure he did not die from the drugs as two other students had done previously at the school. These experiences had pushed her to the edge, causing her to question her career because they had hit her very hard and had weighed heavily on her. After a few days, she had come to the realization as a person and as a teacher that her position was to make sure she did everything possible to affect her students positively, helping them to make the best choices they could to be successful and responsible.

She ended the Real Talk by connecting it back to norms in her classroom. Her experiences with her former students and many other personal experiences were the reasons behind the rules in her class, including the one about not laying their heads down in class. These rules were created to help and benefit her students. After she concluded, her students asked many sincere questions about the experiences she had shared.

After her Real Talk, the class atmosphere was positive, something she had rarely encountered after going over classroom rules. Several weeks later, the teacher further reflected on this specific Real Talk. She noted that this was the best class she had ever had regarding students putting their heads down in her class. It was hardly an issue at all, and she no longer had to have discussions with her students about why they couldn't sleep in her class. She felt strongly that the Real Talk helped her students see her perspective on this particular issue. She wasn't just a grouchy teacher who was giving them a hard time. She also felt far more connected to this class than she had with previous classes in her many years of teaching.

# *Appendix I*

## *Examples of Real Talk Themes*

I used these four themes with my classes and have provided a summary of the Real Talk experiences I shared with students. However, teachers using Real Talk need to tailor their themes to the terministic screens of their students and to their own personal experiences, or use the resources discussed throughout the book to create authentic, relevant Real Talks.

## VICTIMIZATION

Mrs. F, a former teacher of mine, blamed me for throwing an apple into her classroom when I walked past her classroom on my way to the school counseling office. Two male students ran past me and turned a corner out of sight. When I turned to see what they were running from, Mrs. F exited her room and began to yell at me: "I know you threw the apple! People saw you throw the apple! Come here now! I am taking you to the Vice Principal's office!" I told her it wasn't me. She said, "There is no one else walking in the hall other than you!" I tied this experience of feeling victimized by this teacher to receiving consequences for the actions of someone else. Students then shared their experiences with victimization.

## HAPPINESS

I relayed my experience of watching my first group of HEP students pass the GED tests. Witnessing all of the hard work that they had put into their studies and the personal struggles that they had to overcome to get to the end of the program, I felt extreme happiness when I saw them finish the program and get their GED diplomas. I tied this experience to happiness being an emotion most people feel. Students then shared experiences that had made them happy in life.

# FRUSTRATION

I recalled a police officer speaking to me in a condescending, disrespectful manner. I was a passenger in a car with a group of friends driving down a major boulevard in Los Angeles. We were pulled over by officers from the sheriff's department. One of the deputies who had surrounded us asked us to exit the vehicle one by one. One deputy explained that they had pulled us over because the car was in violation of a California vehicle law. They impounded the car and detained my friend, the driver. I was told to find a way home. I asked if I could get back in the car to get my wallet and was told no. I explained that my wallet was in the car and that, without my wallet, I could not get a taxi or pay bus fare to get home. The officer said that it was not his problem and that if I did not walk away, I would be arrested. I explained the frustration I felt because I could not do anything about the sheriff's deputy acting in that manner. I tied it to the fact that we can experience frustration in many different places within society. I then asked students to share any of their experiences of frustration.

# TRIUMPH

After attending community college for two years, I had accrued all of the credits needed not only to transfer to a university but also to earn an associate's degree. I remembered the feeling when I received the letter of congratulations for completing my community college degree, which I would soon receive in the mail. I was extremely happy and felt I had truly triumphed in my life. I had achieved something that many people thought I could never achieve. I tied this experience to my students completing and achieving their GEDs and explained that we would feel this triumphant feeling together as a group at the end of the semester.

# *Appendix J*

## *Bridge Project Packet*

Name: _____ Hour: _____

## MINI LESSON 1: CENTER OF MASS AND GRAVITY

Gravity is: _____

_____

_____

_____

_____

_____

_____ .

_____

Center of mass is: _____

_____

_____

_____

_____

_____

_____ .

## Finding Center of Mass

| | | |
|---|---|---|
| | | |
| | | |

When I stand
straight up
my center of
mass is . . .

When I stand on
my left foot
my center of
mass is . . .

When I lean against
a wall with the left
part of my body my
center of mass is . . .

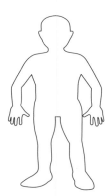

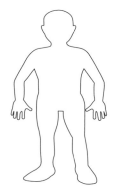

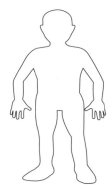

Stability is: _____

_____

_____ .

The _____ a building is, the _____ the
base must be because:

_____

_____ .

Draw a building that would be stable and a building that would not be stable, and then write one sentence for each to explain why:

| Stable Building | Not Stable Building |
|---|---|
| | |
| Explanation: <br><br> _____ <br><br> _____ <br><br> _____ <br><br> _____ <br><br> _____ | Explanation: <br><br> _____ <br><br> _____ <br><br> _____ <br><br> _____ <br><br> _____ |

To ensure the _____ amount of weight is held by the bridge, where should the weight be placed? _____

If the weight is not placed in the middle, what will happen? (Use two vocabulary words that we learned today and give two sentences.)

_____

_____

_____

_____

Explain how you will use what we learned today to make the best bridge.

_____

_____

_____

Draw a sample bridge and show where the center of mass will be.

## MINI LESSON 2: SYMMETRY AND POWER OF THE TRIANGLE

Draw three images you created on http://www.mathsisfun.com/geometry/symmetry-artist.html.

| y = x axis | Origin | x axis |
| --- | --- | --- |

Symmetry is: _____

_____

_____.

Give four reasons why symmetry is important in structures.

1. _____

2. _____

3. _____

4. _____

Our bridges must be symmetric _____ and

_____.

Why is symmetry important to the design of our bridges? _____

_____

_____

_____

Draw a sketch of a bridge that is symmetric and one that is not.

| Symmetric Bridge Design | Non-Symmetric Bridge Design |
|---|---|
| | |

# TRIANGLES

Prediction: I think the strongest shape to use in a bridge is _____.

I think this because _____.

A _____ is the strongest structural shape there is.

This is because _____

_____

_____

_____.

**Creating Shapes**

Draw three shapes you created with the cardstock and fasteners.

Circle the weak points in the structure.

Redraw the shape you made after you made it stronger with triangles.

| Shape 1 | Shape 2 | Shape 3 |
|---|---|---|
| | | |
| Shape 1 With Triangles | Shape 2 With Triangles | Shape 3 With Triangles |
| | | |

Why are your shapes stronger now that you have added triangles? How do you know they are stronger?

_____

_____

_____

How can you incorporate triangles into your bridge design?

_____

_____

## DESIGN OF THE BRIDGE

Before you start building your bridge, you must sketch a draft of what you hope your bridge will look like. Remember the bridge must span a distance of 40 cm. Try measuring the width of a Popsicle stick and determine how many you will need for the base of the bridge.

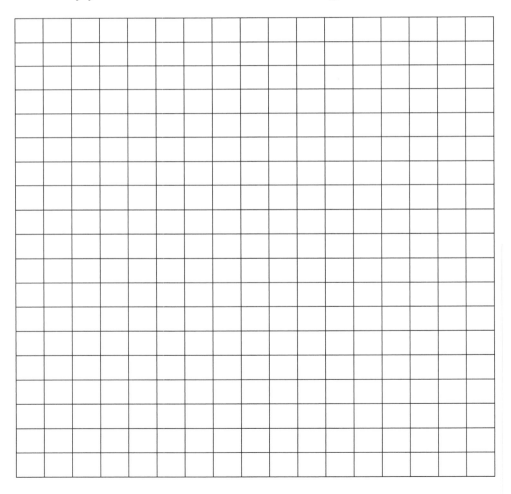

# FORMAL COLLEGE EXPERIMENT REPORT

**Objective:** _____

_____

_____

_____

_____

_____

_____

**Materials:** _____

_____

**Hypothesis:** _____

_____

_____

_____

_____

_____

_____

**Procedure**

_____

_____

_____

_____

_____

_____

**Calculations**

One Popsicle stick is _____ wide and _____ long.

I need _____ Popsicle sticks to make sure my bridge is long enough.

Shapes I will use in my bridge and how I will use them:

## Graphs

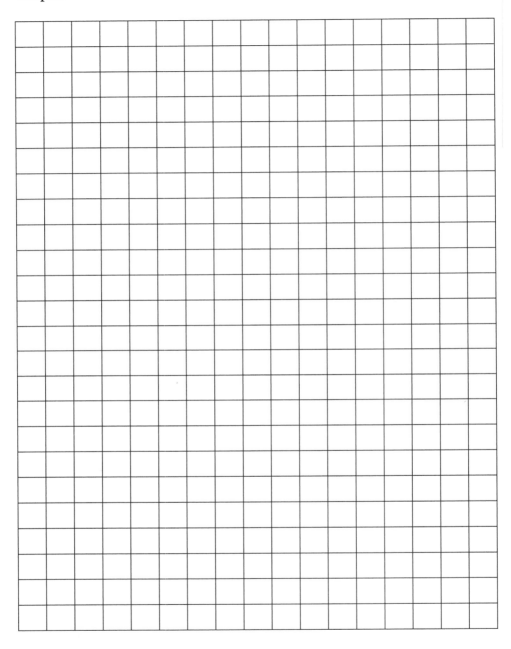

## Analysis

_____
_____
_____
_____
_____
_____

## Conclusion

_____
_____
_____

My hypothesis was _____

_____

because _____

_____ .

Revision and Reflection: Every good scientist and mathematician looks back on his or her design critically and thinks about how the design could be better.
Our challenge: In this class, we have so many brilliant brains, so if we put them together, could we as a class come up with an even better bridge that can withstand 100 pounds?
What do we need to do?

**Peer to Peer Evaluation**

| Group | Picture | I think this bridge will hold ___ because . . . (minimum one sentence) | This bridge is good because . . . (minimum one sentence) | Rating 1—10 (1 lowest, 10 highest) |
|---|---|---|---|---|
| | | | | |
| | | | | |
| | | | | |
| | | | | |

# *Appendix K*

## *Alternative Lesson on Congruent Triangles*

This lesson was created by the math teacher I spoke of in Chapter 11, "Training and Feedback." This is an excellent example of a clear difference between a Real Talk (see Appendix D) and an alternative lesson. The Real Talk and alternative lesson both focused on congruent triangles and assumptions but were used according to how each is defined and meant to be used in the classroom.

The alternative lesson she created focused on the highly publicized murder case of Casey Anthony. Even though this case was very popular around the country, the teacher did not assume that all her students knew about the case and, thus, introduced the case as the starting point of the alternative lesson. She purposely selected the following story because she knew it would strike a chord or resonate with her class, given the information she had learned about their terministic screens. She introduced the case by showing a YouTube clip that summarized the murder trial. Occasionally, instead of showing the video, she would hand out a one-page article highlighting the case and would elaborate on the details of the story.

The Casey Anthony murder trial was highly controversial around the country. Casey Anthony was accused of murdering her two-year-old daughter, Caylee.[1] Despite the enormous amount of evidence and the numerous expert witnesses testifying in the attempt to convict Casey Anthony of murdering her daughter, that was not the outcome. The media coverage for this case was massive and widespread, with many people within the media and public sector having very strong opinions on the matter of Casey Anthony's guilt. When Casey Anthony was acquitted by

---

[1]Lizette Alvarez, "Casey Anthony Not Guilty in Slaying of Daughter," *New York Times*, July 5, 2011, http://www.nytimes.com/2011/07/06/us/06casey.html?pagewanted=all&_r=0.

the jury, the media and country erupted with outcries that Casey Anthony was getting away with murder. By the end of the introduction of the murder trial, all of the students were familiar with the details of the story and were asked about their opinions on the case.

The teacher highlighted the public opinion component of how an overwhelming majority of the public considered her guilty. She followed this by asking students for their opinions on the matter. Many students shared their perspectives and thoughts on the case and eventually the teacher asked the class, "Why was Casey Anthony acquitted despite public opinion?" Students were captivated by the story; it connected with them, making them not only receptive but also willing to participate. Students began to answer.

The teacher eventually stepped in to tie things directly to the lesson she had for the students. She shared that although there was evidence against Casey Anthony, the case illustrated the importance of having the right evidence. She then introduced congruent triangles and the appropriate information to answer questions correctly. She transitioned by explaining that having the correct evidence is a crucial component in proving that two triangles are congruent. She explained that it does not matter if the two triangles look the same (heck, maybe they are the same!), if that information isn't given or if the right pieces of information aren't given, no one can prove that the two triangles are congruent. She followed this by handing out the following assignment.

## Congruent Triangles Investigation

**Name:** _____

You are a lawyer at an important math law firm that helps prove whether or not two triangles are congruent. Remember, in order for two triangles to be congruent, all of their corresponding sides must be congruent and all of their corresponding angles must be congruent!

There are a few shortcuts you can use to prove that two triangles are congruent. You can win the trial if you can prove one of the five following triangle congruencies apply to your case:

**SSS:** _____

**SAS:** _____

**AAS:** _____

**ASA:** _____

**RHL:** _____

You may need to collect additional evidence in order to win your case. For each piece of additional evidence you collect, you must be able to back it up in court with a valid mathematical justification! A list of common theorems and properties is attached at the end of this packet.

**Case 1:** Lindsey and Kenzie were both adopted as young triangles. Twenty years later, they met at a party and their resemblance couldn't be denied! After a long discussion, they came to the conclusion that they must be identical twins. Since genetic testing isn't available for triangles, they have come to you to help them prove that they are congruent triangles.

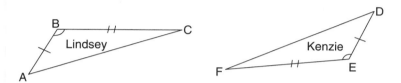

**Facts:** What information is given to you (either in a given statement or information from the diagrams)?

**Evidence:** What information, if any, do you still need to gather? How can you prove that this new information is true?

**Your Conclusion:** What is your conclusion (are the two triangles congruent)? What triangle congruency did you use to make your claim?

**Case 2:** A local storeowner has come to you needing legal representation. One night, his store was robbed. Security cameras recorded the robbery and based on the footage, a local triangle named Jeff is being accused of the robbery. Jeff claims it can't be him, because only some of his features are the same as in the security footage. The storeowner wants you to prove that Jeff is guilty of committing the robbery by proving that Jeff is the same triangle that was captured in the security footage.

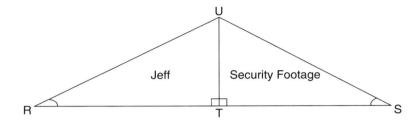

Jeff agrees that his angle $R$ is the same as the angle $S$ in the footage and that both he and the triangle in the footage have the same angle $T$. However, Jeff claims that you can't provide enough additional evidence to prove he is the same triangle in the footage.

**Facts:** What information is given to you (either in a given statement or information from the diagrams)?

**Evidence:** What information, if any, do you still need to gather? How can you prove that this new information is true?

**Your Conclusion:** What is your conclusion (are the two triangles congruent)? What triangle congruency did you use to make your claim?

The judge has asked that you present your evidence in the form of a two-column proof. Fill in the two-column proof below:

| Evidence | Justification |
|---|---|
| 1. | 1. |
| 2. | 2. |
| 3. | 3. |

**Case 3:** Maria is being accused of a crime she claims she didn't commit. A house in her neighborhood was broken into a few nights ago, and a neighbor claimed that she saw Maria sneaking around the backyard. However, Maria has photos of herself at a party that were taken at the same time that the breaking and entering occurred. The neighbor does not believe Maria's alibi and does not think that the triangle in the pictures is Maria. Maria has come to you to help her clear her name and prove that she is the same triangle that is in the picture.

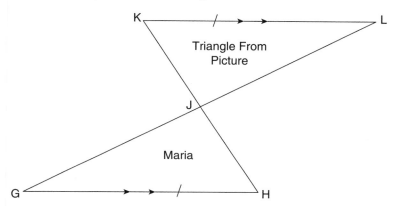

The only information that Maria can give you is that her side $\overline{GH}$ is parallel and congruent to the side $\overline{LK}$ in the picture.

**Facts:** What information is given to you (either in a given statement or information from the diagrams)?

**Evidence:** What information, if any, do you still need to gather? How can you prove that this new information is true?

**Your Conclusion:** What is your conclusion (are the two triangles congruent)? What triangle congruency did you use to make your claim?

# IMPORTANT THEOREMS AND PROPERTIES: USE THESE FOR PROOFS!

**Vertical Angles**

All vertical angles are congruent

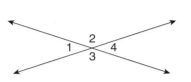

∠1 ≅ ∠4 and ∠2 ≅ ∠3

**Alternate Interior Angles**

If two parallel lines are cut by a transversal, then the pairs of alternate interior angles are congruent.

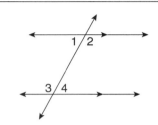

∠1 ≅ ∠4 and ∠2 ≅ ∠3

**Triangle Sum Theorem**

The sum of the measure of the interior angles of a triangle is 180°.

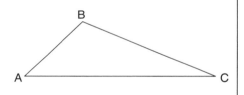

$m\angle A + m\angle B + m\angle C = 180°$

**Corresponding Angles**

If two parallel lines are cut by a transversal, then the pairs of corresponding angles are congruent.

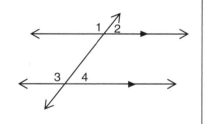

∠1 ≅ ∠3 and ∠2 ≅ ∠4

**Reflexive Property of Congruence**

Any side or angle is congruent to itself.

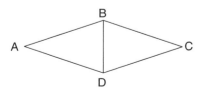

$\overline{BD} \cong \overline{BD}$

**Third Angle Theorem**

If two angles of one triangle are congruent to two angles of another triangle, then the third angles are also congruent.

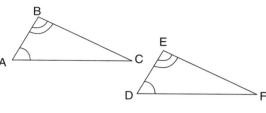

If ∠A ≅ ∠D and ∠B ≅ ∠E, then ∠C ≅ ∠F

# *Appendix L*

## *Alternative Lesson on Federal Courts and the Judicial Branch*

This alternative lesson was used by a teacher in her Civics class to help students learn a topic that she shared they were commonly not interested in learning. According to the teacher, the state standards she was addressing were the following:

- Identify and explain competing arguments about the necessity and purposes of governments (such as protecting inalienable rights, promote the general welfare, resolve conflicts, promote equality, and establish justice for all).
- Analyze the purposes, organization, functions, and processes of the judicial branch as enumerated in Article III of the Constitution.
- Analyze the various levels and responsibilities of courts in the federal and state judicial system, and explain the relationships among them.

More specifically within her lesson, her objectives were the following: Students will be able to

- explain the reason why we have laws,
- explain what courts do,
- explain the difference between state courts and federal courts, and
- explain the difference between original jurisdiction and appellate jurisdiction.

Although these were the overall goals that directly connected to the curriculum, she created the lesson to generate interest and to establish receptiveness to learn from her students.

The teacher had learned from her students' terministic screens that they had a strong inclination toward hip-hop music and the right to say whatever they wanted as part of their everyday lives. The teacher more specifically learned about a few different music artists that the students discussed and felt strongly about. She selected the hip-hop artist Eminem, based on what she had learned from her students. But the teacher went a step further because she had used Real Talk in her class throughout the semester. The students had learned many things about her, and had a strong connection with this teacher. This allowed her to contribute some of her own musical taste, so she included a band that she enjoyed, Metallica, in the alternative lesson as well.

Overall, this alternative lesson worked extremely well for the teacher. She generated tremendous interest, receptiveness, engagement, and effort from her students; and her students learned the necessary material. The teacher shared her excitement and joy in watching her students at risk become so involved in the learning process during this alternative lesson.

She did an excellent job with this alternative lesson. The lesson is very flexible in that the musical artists can be replaced each semester, based on the musical artists the class prefers, while the structure she created can be maintained. Her personal notes on conducting this alternative lesson are given on the following pages.

# ALTERNATIVE LESSON: THE ROLE OF THE FEDERAL COURTS

**Warm-Up Question:** Why do artists swear in their music? Is it really necessary for artists to swear in their music? Why or why not? Do you think they should be sued for their profane music lyrics? Why or why not?

**Introduction:** Play the YouTube clip of Eminem's song, "Love the Way You Lie." I only play the first couple of minutes of the clip because the video is pretty graphic and then he starts swearing. I stop the video about 4 times within that time frame and say, "Inappropriate!" Students get mad at me for judging his appearance in the video (tank top and tattoos). I stop it right after he says, "I can't tell you what is only what it feels like and right now it's a steel knife in my windpipe." I say to the class, "His girlfriend stabbed him? Inappropriate!" Of course, it is symbolism; and the kids try to tell me this, but I stop them, only making them angrier at me for judging him and his music.

## Lesson

1. **Pass out cards to students:** Judge (student); plaintiff (me); defendant (Eminem—student in class); jury (rest of class)

2. **Civil Lawsuit:** Take class through a civil case using Eminem as the defendant while I am the plaintiff, suing him over his music (lyrics).

3. **Ask:** What is the job of courts?

4. **Ask:** If I sue Eminem, what would I be? Plaintiff or defendant? (plaintiff) What would he be? (defendant)

5. *Ms. I v. Eminem (2012):* I am suing Eminem for his profane music. I bring up other lyrics from the song and show other parts of his video as evidence in court.

6. *Ms. I v. Metallica (2011):* Court will use this case as a PRECEDENT (guideline) to determine how they will rule on the *Ike v. Eminem* case. The year before I had sued Metallica for their profane music lyrics.

7. **Original jurisdiction:** State trial court hears first; then the case moves through the state courts (trial, appeal, supreme). If Eminem's lawyers believe he did not receive a fair trial, he will APPEAL.

8. **Appellate jurisdiction:** The appellate court hears the case the second time around. It reviews the facts in the case to determine if the law applied fairly. Did Eminem get a fair trial?

9. **Court decision:** Is Eminem guilty or innocent?

**Closure:** Students take the following quiz over the material presented in the lesson: plaintiff; defendant; judge; jury; original jurisdiction; appellate jurisdiction; precedent.

## Quiz: *Ms. I v. Eminem (2012)*

Directions: Answer the questions below from the case *Ms. I v. Eminem.*

1. If I (Ms. I) sue Eminem because of his lyrics and take him to court, what would he be in this case? (plaintiff or defendant)

2. What would I (Ms. I) be, the plaintiff or defendant, if I sue Eminem?

3. Explain what the judge and the jury would do in this case.

4. There was a similar case a year ago, *Ms. I v. Metallica* (2011), where a law established that all music containing explicit lyrics or content should have a parental advisory label on it. This court case would be used as a _____, or guideline, in the Eminem case above.

5. A trial court will hear this case first because they have _____ jurisdiction.

    A. If Eminem is found guilty and he feels he did not receive a fair trial, what can he do?
    B. What court will hear his case and why?

# *Appendix M*

## *Alternative Lesson on Graphing Different Types of Linear Systems*

For this alternative lesson, I have used another math example. This teacher created a wonderful alternative lesson based on Bernie Madoff. The teacher had approached me after a professional development day with her school and asked if I could help her with topics that would connect to her students. I decided to help her brainstorm, first focusing on her students and what she had learned about them through Real Talk. She mentioned a variety of things, but the thing that jumped out at me the most was their issues with money. She mentioned that her students had strong connections to money: not having any, not having enough, wanting as much as possible, ways to achieve monetary success, and so forth.

With this in mind, I proposed that the teacher use Bernie Madoff as the topic for her lesson. The case was a high-profile and well-publicized case. It was also a very intimate topic based on the crimes committed by Madoff. I suggested she use the angle of the Ponzi scheme that Madoff used to steal $50 billion from people. She was familiar with the case and knew her class far better than I did and felt that my suggestion would work well with her students. Based on our conversation, she created the alternative lesson based on the Bernie Madoff Ponzi scheme.

In her alternative lesson, she first introduced Bernie Madoff and what he did to his investors. She did not assume all of her students knew the story or knew who he was, so she showed the class a YouTube clip.[2] The video was less than five minutes in length. It summarized Bernie Madoff's crime, gave a short explanation of the Ponzi scheme he used to rob his investors, identified the people and companies his crime affected, and included an interview with an elderly couple who lost their entire life savings because of Madoff. After showing the video, she elaborated on what

---

[2]See clip at http://www.youtube.com/watch?v=lzAUUyd-woE&feature=relmfu.

a Ponzi scheme is to make sure that it was clear to her students. She phrased what Madoff did as a "hustle" to rob innocent investors. To connect it directly to her students, as she ended her explanation of the Madoff Ponzi scheme, she asked her students, "How would you feel if you lost everything after an entire life of hard work?" Her students were eager to participate, and many of them answered her question with well-thought-out and profound answers because they could empathize with the victims. Some students even had their own stories of friends or family who had lost their savings or large amounts of money.

Once she felt comfortable with the class participation and with allowing her students to openly share their terministic screens, she transitioned into handing out the following assignment. Later she shared that throughout the entire video and her lecture, her students were entirely engaged. She also shared her excitement with me about being able to create such an effective alternative lesson.

**Types of Systems of Equations**

**Name:** _____

**Problem 1:** Bernie Madoff is scamming money from two people, and he wants to know from which one of them he will earn the most over time:

Bob makes an initial investment of $100 and pays Madoff an additional $300 each month.

Equation: _____

Matt makes an initial investment of $1,000 and pays an additional $150 each month.

Equation: _____

Graph the two equations on the grid below and create a table of values. You may use your graphing calculator for assistance. Use a different color to graph the lines for Bob and Matt.

*HINT!: Adjust your window! $x$ range from 0–10 with an $x$-scl of 1. $y$ range from 0–5000 with a $y$-scl of 500.

| Bob | | | Matt | |
|---|---|---|---|---|
| **X**<br>months | **Y**<br>profit | | **X**<br>months | **Y**<br>profit |
| 0 | | | 0 | |
| 1 | | | 1 | |
| 2 | | | 2 | |
| 3 | | | 3 | |
| 4 | | | 4 | |
| 5 | | | 5 | |
| 6 | | | 6 | |
| 7 | | | 7 | |
| 8 | | | 8 | |
| 9 | | | 9 | |
| 10 | | | 10 | |

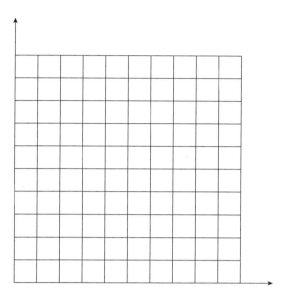

Who is more profitable after 2 months? _____

Who is more profitable after 8 months? _____

At what point will Bob and Matt be equally profitable? _____

Madoff can choose either Bob or Matt to collect money from for one year. Madoff wants to earn as much money as possible. Whom should he choose and why? _____

_____

**Problem 2:** Bernie Madoff has two more people willing to give him money. Each gives him the same amount of money per month, but he collects different start-up fees from each person.

Pearl makes an initial investment of $100 and pays Madoff an additional $300 each month.

Equation: _____

Felicia makes an initial investment of $500 and pays an additional $300 each month.

Equation: _____

Graph the two equations on the grid below and create a table of values. You may use your graphing calculator for assistance. Use a different color to graph the lines for Pearl and Felicia.

*HINT!: Adjust your window! $x$ range from 0–10 with an $x$-scl of 1. $y$ range from 0–5000 with a $y$-scl of 500.

| Pearl | | | Felicia | |
|---|---|---|---|---|
| X months | Y profit | | X months | Y profit |
| 0 | | | 0 | |
| 1 | | | 1 | |
| 2 | | | 2 | |
| 3 | | | 3 | |
| 4 | | | 4 | |
| 5 | | | 5 | |
| 6 | | | 6 | |
| 7 | | | 7 | |
| 8 | | | 8 | |
| 9 | | | 9 | |
| 10 | | | 10 | |

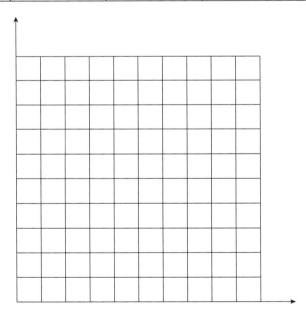

Who is more profitable after 2 months? _____

Who is more profitable after 8 months? _____

Will Pearl ever be more profitable than Felicia? Why or why not? _____

_____

**Problem 3:** Jake and Deshawn are eager to pool their money and make an investment with Madoff. Madoff has offered them two choices:

**Choice A:** Madoff will collect a total of $300 from Jake and Deshawn, with Jake paying in increments of $75 (i.e., $75, $150, $225 . . . ) and Deshawn paying in increments of $50.

Equation: _____

**Choice B:** Madoff will collect a total of $600 from Jake and Deshawn, with Jake paying in increments of $150 and Deshawn paying in increments of $100.

Equation: _____

Graph the two equations. Use a different color for Choice A and Choice B. *HINT!: Graph by finding the $x$ and $y$ intercepts for each equation!

What are three different combinations of money Jake and Deshawn could pay for Choice A?

_____

_____

_____

What are three different combinations of money Jake and Deshawn could pay for Choice B?

_____

_____

_____

Let $x$ be the number of increments that Jake contributes and $y$ be the increments that Deshawn contributes. Is there a combination of increments that would be a possible solution for Choice A yet would NOT work for Choice B? Explain:

_____

_____

_____

# *Appendix N*

## *Alternative Lesson on Public Speaking Anxiety*

In this lesson, the teacher who teaches technology, English, and public speaking (speech) classes was attempting to create a lesson to help his public speaking students. The students in his class were typically anxious when it came to public speaking. This led many of them to act out in a variety of ways and not to take the work in class seriously or even to put forth any effort in the class. After conducting a Real Talk during the first week of class, he followed this by introducing an alternative lesson that same week. The alternative lesson was very creative, using zombies to address public speaking anxiety. The teacher's objectives in this alternative lesson were to create open communication with individual students and between the students and the teacher, and to introduce the uncomfortable subject of anxiety. In using this introductory alternative lesson, he was also attempting to overcome the traditional resistance he encountered with his students when beginning this class. The outcome he desired for himself and his students was to give his students a way to examine their anxiety about the course to allow them to begin working toward creating and executing speeches in the class. He wanted his students to begin the class on a positive note by using a lesson that shows the issue of anxiety connected to public speaking as a normal process in this particular class. Thus, he set the tone for the class in the first lesson: knowing and accepting that if they feel any anxiety with public speaking, they must address it before they can move forward in the class.

The teacher learned very quickly in the semester that his students liked zombies, and the teacher also liked zombies. He used this common ground as the launching pad to his lesson. He did not begin the lesson speaking about speeches or public speaking, avoiding that until the very end of his lesson. Instead, he went to the chalkboard and wrote the word *zombies* large enough for everyone in class to read. After he wrote the word on the board, he announced to his class that they were beginning class by talking about zombies, and the lesson began.

## Lesson Overview

After writing the word on the board and telling the class they are going to talk about zombies, the teacher talked a little bit about his love of zombies: zombie movies, comics, video games, and television shows. He then asked the students what they knew about zombies. This began a dialogue. After they had offered some information, the teacher gave a history of zombies. He talked about voodoo zombies and what they are. He specifically covered how they were used as a tool against an individual or small groups of people, explaining that, in this form, they were not scary unless the person was one of the people the zombie was brought back to kill.

The teacher then talked about George A. Romero, the creator of the current concept of a zombie. When he was creating the original *Night of the Living Dead* in 1968, Romero wanted zombies to be scarier. He looked at the concept of tribal warfare and the practice of cannibalism. The teacher explained that non–Jeffery Dahmer–style cannibals do not eat their victims for nourishment. Rather, it is a form of psychological warfare. The teacher then introduced the students to the idea of fighting a war in which you know your enemy is going to eat you. This is the idea that Romero added to zombies. Just by adding cannibalism to zombies, he made them into a "universal fear," something everyone is scared of.

At this point, the teacher began to talk about public speaking. He communicated that they all talk to people every day. They talk one-on-one, in small groups, over the phone, and through digital communication. The teacher then talked about adding public speaking to communication. He then compared adding cannibalism to zombies with adding public to speaking, which also creates universal fear. At this point, the students were usually ready to start examining why they were fearful or apprehensive about public speaking. The teacher usually had them write about it, share their writing with a partner or a group, and then share as a class.

# *Appendix O*

## *Alternative Lesson Topics and Summaries*

### POWERPOINT PICTURE VIEWING

Create a PowerPoint—or Keynote, Prezi, or whichever presentation software you prefer—that defines the concepts being covered in class, and allow students to be a part of the presentation. For example, create slides that show students a variety of pictures with no words. Ask students what each picture symbolizes to them and why.

### SILENTLY VIEWING YOUTUBE CLIPS

Carefully select a variety of YouTube clips and show them to the class without volume. Ask the class to make inferences about what is being discussed or what is happening in the clips based on the people's body language.

### WATCHING MOVIE CLIPS

Select scenes in movies that show the personality, physical appearance, or behavior of a character. Ask students to analyze the character.

### WEEKEND EXPERIENCE

Have students write about what they did over the weekend. After they finish, have a few students discuss their activities through class discussion and questioning. Then ask questions connecting these activities to the concepts being learned in class.

## A PIECE OF THEMSELVES

Have students choose one or two of their favorite songs and play the songs for the class. They then answer two questions for the class: What is the meaning of the song? What does the song mean to them?

## READING *MALCOLM X* BY ALEX HALEY

Assign the introduction, epilogue, and all chapters to individual students to read. If there are more students than the available chapters, assign two students per chapter. Allow students two weeks to do the reading and plan a presentation of their portions to the class. The class must depend on one another to understand the entire book. Once the presentations are completed, have the class watch the movie *Malcolm X* by Spike Lee.

## GROUP WORK

These kinds of activities may be done by partners (two students) or small groups (three to five students). Teachers may add a factor of competition between groups to motivate students even further.

- Solve a riddle.
- Create a short story.
- Create a unique poem.
- Complete study guides or worksheets.
- Complete peer editing exercises.

## STUDENTS AS TEACHERS

After initial instruction, teachers can ask students to teach the class concepts as a way to reinforce instruction and evaluate understanding of those concepts.

- Have students draw a scenario or representation of the concept on the board. Have the rest of the class try to figure out what each drawing depicts. Then have the students who drew the scenarios explain them to the class or elaborate on the class's understanding of the picture.
- Have students explain to the class what their neighborhoods are like using figurative language. Students should focus on the differences between their neighborhoods and other neighborhoods, the things that make their neighborhood unique.

# *Appendix P*

## *Games*

The following games were created through the initiation and help of my students. This was not an intended outcome but more a result of the connections and success established with my students.

## QUIZ BOWL

Develop a series of questions based on the material being studied. Project the questions on the whiteboard or any other board used to project images. Students ring a bell to indicate they can answer the question. The first person who rings in answers. Various point systems can be used. Students can do this individually or as teams. Competitions can be ongoing or separate. Teachers may also decide to award small prizes, depending on the level of intrinsic motivation students exhibit.

## BATTLESHIP

Divide the class into two teams to play the classic game of Battleship™. Teams score a direct hit on the opposing team by getting a correct answer to a question asked (provided verbally or projected on an overhead screen). If the answering team does not get the correct answer, the opposing team gets a direct hit on the answering team.

## JEOPARDY

Split the class into two teams. Have them compete in answering questions prepared for various categories selected from the material being studied. Follow the game pattern of the television show *Jeopardy* using questions relevant to your class.

## WHITEBOARD COMPETITIONS

Have two to five students go to the board at the same time. Have the students write on the board their answers to questions posed verbally. The first student to write down the correct answer on the board earns a point for that student's team.

Another version is to have the student at the board write down the team's answer to the question, which usually speeds up the competition.

# Bibliography

"1965 Alabama Literacy Test." *Social Education* 60, no. 6 (1996): 340.

Alliance for Excellent Education. *The High Cost of High School Dropouts: What the Nation Pays for Inadequate High Schools.* Washington, DC: 2011.

Anderson, Elijah. *Code of the Street: Decency, Violence, and the Moral Life of the Inner City.* New York: W.W. Norton, 1999.

Anderson, M. L., and H. F. Taylor. *Sociology: The Essentials.* Belmont, CA: Thomson Higher Education, 2012.

Armstrong, Thomas. *Multiple Intelligences in the Classroom.* Alexandria, VA: Association for Supervision and Curriculum Development, 2000.

Billings-Ladson, Gloria. "Towards a Theory of Culturally Relevant Pedagogy." *American Educational Research Journal* 32, no. 3 (1995): 465–491.

Blumer, Herbert. *Symbolic Interactionism: Perspectives and Method.* Los Angeles: University of California Press, 1969.

Cammarota, Julio. "Disappearing in the Houdini Education: The Experience of Race and Invisibility." *Multicultural Education* 14 (2006): 2–10.

Cassidy, Wanda, and Anita Bates. "Drop-Outs and Push Outs: Finding Hope at a School That Actualizes the Ethic of Care." *American Journal of Education* 112 (2005): 66–102.

Chang, Heewon. *Autoethnography as Method.* Walnut Creek, CA: Left Coast Press, 2009.

Cohen, Albert K. *Delinquent Boy: The Culture of the Gang.* Glencoe, IL: The Free Press, 1955.

Crosnoe, Robert, Monica Kirkpatrick Johnson, and Glen H. Elder, Jr. "Intergenerational Bonding in School: The Behavioral and Contextual Correlates of Student–Teacher Relationships." *Sociology of Education* 77 (2004): 60–81.

Downey, Douglas B., and Shana Pribesh. "When Race Matters: Teachers' Evaluations of Students' Classroom Behavior." *Sociology of Education* 77 (2004): 267–282.

Erera, Pauline. *Family Diversity: Continuity and Change in the Contemporary Family.* Thousand Oaks, CA: Sage, 2002.

Freire, Paulo. *Pedagogy of the Oppressed.* New York: Continuum, 1970.

Gosa, Travis L., and Karl Alexander. "Family (Dis)Advantage and the Educational Prospects of Better Off African American Youth: How Race Still Matters." *Teachers College Record* 109 (2007): 285–321.

Hallinan, Maureen T. "Teacher Influences on Students' Attachment to School." *Sociology of Education* 81 (2008): 271–283.

Hernandez, Paul. *Alternative Pedagogy: Empowering Teachers Through Real Talk* (Doctoral dissertation, Michigan State University, 2010). Retrieved from ProQuest.

Hernandez, Paul. "College 101: Introducing At-Risk Students to Higher Education." *NEA Higher Education Journal* Fall (2011): 77–89.

Hernandez, Paul. "MSU Student Backgrounds: Poverty, Discrimination, and Dropping Out of School." *Michigan Sociological Review* 24 (2010): 97–129.

Horvat, Erin Mcnamara, Elliot B. Weininger, and Annette Lareau. "From Social Ties to Social Capital: Class Differences in the Relations Between Schools and Parent Networks." *American Educational Research Journal* 40 (2003): 319–351.

Lareau, Annete. *Unequal Childhoods: Class, Race, and Family Life.* Berkeley: University of California Press, 2003.

Leard, Wishart, and Brett Lashua. "Popular Media, Critical Pedagogy, and Inner City Youth." *Canadian Journal of Education* 29, no. 1 (2006): 244–264.

Lee, Sook-Jung, and Natasha K. Bowen. "Parent Involvement, Cultural Capital, and the Achievement Gap Among Elementary School Children." *American Educational Research Journal* 43 (2006): 193–218.

Lee, Valeria, and David T. Burkham. "Dropping Out of High School: The Role of School Organization and Structure." *American Educational Research Journal* 40 (2003): 353–393.

Lewis-Peterson, Sonja, and Lisa M. Bratton. "Perceptions of 'Acting Black' Among African American Teens: Implications of Racial Dramaturgy for Academic and Social Achievement." *The Urban Review* 36 (2004): 81–100.

Macedo, Donald. Introduction to *Pedagogy of the Oppressed*, by Paulo Freire, 11–27. New York: Continuum, 2000.

Marcus, Robert F., and Joanne Sanders-Reio. "The Influence of Attachment on School Completion." *School Psychology Quarterly* 16 (2001): 427–444.

Mastropieri, Margo A., and Thomas E. Scruggs. "Promoting Inclusion in Secondary Classrooms. *Learning Disability Quarterly* 24, no. 4 (2001): 265–274.

Meisels, Samuel J., H. Harrington, P. McMahon, M. Dictelmiller, & J. Jablon. *Thinking Like a Teacher: Using Observational Assessment to Improve Teaching and Learning.* Boston: Allyn and Bacon, 2002.

Meyer, Joan. *How Teachers Can Reach the Disadvantaged: Relating to the Students, Teaching the Students, and Attitudes Towards the Students.* University Park: Pennsylvania State University, Institute of Human Resources, 1968.

Mojica, Leonisa. "Reiterations in ESL Learners' Academic Papers: Do they Contribute to Lexical Cohesiveness?" *The Asia-Pacific Education Research* 15, no. 1 (2006): 105–125.

Muller, Chandra. "The Role of Caring in the Teacher–Student Relationship for At Risk Students." *Sociological Inquiry* 71, no. 2 (2001): 241–255.

Nash, Gary, and Julie Roy Jeffrey G., eds. *The American People: Creating a Nation and a Society.* New York: Longman, 2001.

Northcutt, Ellen, Julie Higgins, and Sarah Combs. *Steck-Vaughn GED Language Arts, Reading.* Austin, TX: Steck-Vaughn, 2002.

Ogbu, John, and Herbert Simmons. "Voluntary and Involuntary Minorities: A Cultural-Ecological Theory of School Performance with Some Implications for Education." *Anthropology and Education Quarterly* 29 (1998): 155–188.

Ogle, Donna M. *Critical Issue: Rethinking Learning for Students at Risk.* Centennial, CO: North Central Regional Education Laboratory, 1997. Retrieved April 5, 2010, from http://www.ncrel.org/sdrs /areas/issues/students/atrisk/at700.htm.

Papachristos, Andrew V. "Gang World." *Carnegie Endowment for International Peace* 147 (2005): 48–55.

Pienda-Gonzales, Julio Antonio, Jose Carols Nunez, Soledad Gonzalez-Pumariega, Luis Alvarez, Cristina Roces, and Marta Garcia. "A Structural Equation Model of Parental Involvement, Motivational and Aptitudinal Characteristics, and Academic Achievement." *The Journal of Experimental Education* 70 (2002): 257–287.

Rockler, Naomi R. "Race, Whiteness, 'Lightness,' and Relevance: African American and European American Interpretations of Jump Start and The Boondocks." *Critical Studies in Media Communication* 19 (2002): 398–418.

"Scene 20" in *Braveheart*, DVD. Directed by Mel Gibson. Los Angeles: Paramount Studios, 1995.

Sebelius, Kathleen. "Annual Update of the HHS Poverty Guidelines." *Federal Registry* 78 (2013): 5182–5183.

Smith, Deborah L., and Brian J. Smith. "Perceptions of Violence: The Views of Teachers Who Left Urban Schools." *The High School Journal* 89, no. 3 (2006): 34–43.

Stormont, Melissa, and Cathy Newman Thomas. *Simple Strategies for Teaching Children at Risk.* Thousand Oaks, CA: Corwin, 2014.

Willis, Paul. *Learning to Labor: How Working Class Kids Get Working Class Jobs.* New York: Columbia University, 1977.

Winterowd, Ross. "Kenneth Burke: An Annotated Glossary of His Terministic Screen and a 'Statistical' Survey of His Major Concepts." *Rhetoric Society Quarterly* 15, no. 3/4 (1985): 145–177.

Zinn, Howard. *A People's History of the United States: 1492–Present.* New York: Harper Perennial, 1995.

# *Index*

Acting Latino, 32
Active listening skill, 8
Adaptability, 62–63
Adversity talk, 133–135
Alternative lessons:
    Bridge Project Packet, 150–160
    congruent triangles, 161–167
    for History, 107–110
    for Language, 113–115
    for Mathematics, 110–113, 161–167,
        171–177
    graphing linear systems, 171–177
    implementation guidelines, 105–107
    judicial system, 169–172
    lesson examples, 107–115
    public speaking anxiety, 179–180
    Real Talk examples, 150–180
    teacher feedback, 118–119
    teacher training, 104–115
    terministic screens, 66–69, 104–105
    "The Me You Don't Know," 68–69
Appropriate pace component:
    defined, 13
    dialogue implementation, 55–56
Assumptions talk, 136–137
Authenticity talk, 144–145

Battleship game, 183
Bridge Project Packet lesson, 150–160

Case study:
    academic results, 24, 40–44
    acting Latino, 32
    disciplinary issues, 35–37
    discrimination experience, 34
    dropout reasons, 37–40
    family history, 26–29
    foreign-born parents, 26
    gang identity, 31, 33

    inception of, 25–26
    linguistic preference, 27
    parental education, 27–28
    parental income, 28–29
    parental length-of-stay in U.S., 27$f$
    past school experiences, 33–37
    poverty-level households, 28–29
    research program, 24, 25–26
    single-mother households, 29
    student ages, 30
    student-at-risk label, 33–34
    student birth place, 30–31
    student participants, 26–40
    student self-identities, 30–33
    thug identity, 31, 33
Clarity component:
    defined, 12–13
    dialogue implementation, 50–51
Classroom norms talk, 146–147
Congruent triangles lesson,
    161–167

Dialogue process:
    maximizing engagement, 46–47
    mutual respect, 46
    problem-posing approach, 12
    Real Talk approach, 11–12
    relating to students, 47–48

Effort, 64–65
Empowerment talk, 140–143
Enthusiasm component:
    defined, 13
    dialogue implementation, 54–55

Flexibility:
    defined, 17–18
    Real Talk implementation, 60–62
    teacher training, 91

Freire, Paulo, 8, 10–11
Frustration theme, 149

Games, 183–184
General Educational Development (GED)
    exam, 6–8, 24–25, 40–44
Graphing lesson, 172–178
Group work, 182

Haley, A., 182
Happiness theme, 148
High school dropouts:
    rates of, 4
    reasons for, 37–40
History lesson, 107–110

Jeopardy game, 183
Judicial system lesson, 168–171

Language lesson, 113–115

Madoff, Bernie, 172–178
*Malcolm X* (Haley), 182
Mastropieri, Margo, 8, 10–11
Mathematics lesson:
    building bridges, 110–113
    congruent triangles, 161–167
    graphing, 172–178
Maximized engagement
        component:
    defined, 13–14
    dialogue implementation, 56–58
    teacher training, 91–92
Meyer, Joan, 8, 10–11
Michigan State University High
        School Equivalency Program
        (MSU HEP), 5, 6–8
    *See also* Case study
Movie clips, 181

Pedagogy defined, 10
Pedagogy of Real Talk:
    active listening skill, 8
    General Educational Development
        (GED) exam, 6–8
    high school dropout rates, 4
    implementation challenge, 121–125
    negative school experiences, 1–2
    Real Talk approach, 8–9
    research background, 5–6
    research program, 6–8
    students at risk, 2–4
    *See also* Real Talk approach

*Pedagogy of the Oppressed* (Freire), 11
Personal challenges talk, 138–139
Piece-of-themselves topic, 182
Ponzi scheme, 172–178
PowerPoint picture viewing, 181
Public speaking lesson, 179–180

Quiz Bowl, 183

Reading assignment, 182
Real Talk approach:
    active listening skill, 8
    adaptability, 62–63
    benefits of, 21–23
    dialogue process, 11–12
    diverse classroom settings, 85–87
    effort, 64–65
    flexibility, 17–18, 60–62
    main concepts, 8–9
    pedagogy defined, 10
    Real Talk discussions, 18–20, 69–76,
        92–101
    S.C.R.E.A.M. variables, 12–14, 17–18,
        48–58, 91
    social constructionism, 15–16
    sociological theory, 15
    strategic implementation of, 20–21
    successful teacher characteristics, 14, 91
    symbolic interactionism, 15–16
    terministic screens, 17, 66–69
    theoretical foundations, 10–14
Real Talk discussions:
    academic example, 98–101
    defined, 18–20
    effects of, 73–76
    maintaining student
        connections, 101–103
    process steps, 94–98
    structure of, 70–72
    teacher feedback, 116–118
    teacher training, 92–101
    themes for, 93–94
Real Talk examples:
    adversity talk, 133–135
    alternative lessons, 150–180
    assumptions talk, 136–137
    authenticity talk, 144–145
    Battleship game, 183
    Bridge Project Packet lesson, 150–160
    classroom norms talk, 146–147
    congruent triangles lesson, 161–167
    empowerment talk, 140–143
    frustration theme, 149

games, 183–184
graphing lesson, 172–178
group work, 182
happiness theme, 148
introduction to, 126–127
Jeopardy game, 183
judicial system lesson, 168–171
lesson topics/summaries, 181–182
movie clips, 181
personal challenges talk, 138–139
piece-of-themselves topic, 182
PowerPoint picture viewing, 181
public speaking lesson, 179–180
Quiz Bowl, 183
reading assignment, 182
sample Real Talks, 128–147
students-as-teachers, 182
symbolism talk, 128–130
triumph theme, 149
victimization theme, 148
weekend experiences, 181
whiteboard competitions, 184
"Who I Am" talk, 131–132
YouTube clips, 181
Real Talk failures:
    case of Jessie, 79–80
    case of LB, 81–82
    case of PB, 77–79
    professional challenges, 82–84
Redundancy component:
    defined, 13
    dialogue implementation, 51–54

S.C.R.E.A.M. variables:
    appropriate pace, 13, 55–56
    clarity, 12–13, 50–51
    enthusiasm, 13, 54–55
    maximized engagement,
        13–14, 56–58
    Real Talk approach, 12–14, 17–18,
        48–58, 91
    redundancy, 13, 51–54
    structure, 12, 48–50
    teacher training, 91
Scruggs, Thomas, 8, 10–11
Social constructionism, 15–16
Sociological theory, 15

Structure component:
    defined, 12
    dialogue implementation, 48–50
Student-as-teacher, 181
Student-at-risk defined, 2–4
Successful teacher characteristics, 14, 91
Symbolic interactionism, 15–16
Symbolism talk, 128–130

Teacher feedback:
    alternative lessons, 118–119
    Real Talk discussions, 116–118
    Real Talk results, 119–120
    terministic screens, 118
Teacher training:
    academic example, 98–101
    alternative lessons, 104–115
    classroom observation, 90
    feedback for, 116–120
    first training session, 89–90
    flexibility, 91
    maintaining student
        connections, 101–103
    maximized engagement
        component, 91–92
    Real Talk approach, 91–92
    Real Talk discussions, 92–101
    Real Talk process, 94–98
    Real Talk themes, 93–94
    S.C.R.E.A.M. variables, 91
    structural strategy, 88–90
    successful teacher characteristics, 91
    volunteer versus mandatory, 88–89
Terministic screens:
    alternative lessons, 66–69, 104–105
    defined, 17
    teacher feedback, 118
"The Me You Don't Know" lesson, 68–69
Triumph theme, 149

Victimization theme, 148

Weekend experiences, 181
Whiteboard competitions, 184
"Who I Am" talk, 131–132

YouTube clips, 172–173, 181

CORWIN
A SAGE Company

Helping educators make the greatest impact

**CORWIN HAS ONE MISSION:** to enhance education through intentional professional learning.

We build long-term relationships with our authors, educators, clients, and associations who partner with us to develop and continuously improve the best evidence-based practices that establish and support lifelong learning.